MW00532733

~~Never~~ Always Bite Off More than You Can Chew

Michael Paulk

TABLE OF CONTENTS

To my mom and dad, Bud and Barbara,
For always loving and supporting me.

To my brothers, Howard and Darryl,
For always getting me in and out of trouble!

To my daughter Mychael,
You are the greatest gift that God could ever bless me with.
I love you eternally!

And most of all, to my beautiful wife Angie.
My life truly began the day I met you and
I promise to love you for all time.
Thank you for always believing in me and
pushing me to be my very best!

PREFACE: "BORN TO BE WILD"

Steppenwolf; 1969

Rocker, Ranger, Broker, Boxer

I was a rocker before I was a ranger and a broker before I was a boxer. Before we get ahead of ourselves, though, you should know I want to sell you something. It is something you've wanted your whole life, even if you didn't realize it until right this second. It's the most precious thing in the world, but not everyone gives it the consideration it deserves.

What I want to sell you, is you.

I want you to be the best possible version of yourself you can possibly be, and no one but yourself can get you there. Now whether you think this is a scratch-and-dent sale or a deluxe, luxury purchase is beside the point. At some time, somewhere, you were sold a lie. It might be the unconscious lies a well-meaning parent tells their offspring, the unconscious lies of cognitive bias, or the intentional lies of thieves and cheats, but our heads can get stuffed full of it. If we are ever going to reach our goals, achieve our dreams, and rise to the top, it is only going to happen through our own hard work.

That's why it is so important to know we are working in the right direction.

In my life, I've had the benefit of a loving dad who gave me such lifelong, resonating advice. Most of his words and advice still echo in my memory decades later. Technically, he's my stepdad. However, I have always left the "step" part off because he's the only father I've ever had. He stepped up and raised me and my older brother as his own, and I'm a better man for it. I know not everyone has had the benefit of an amazing set of parents like I have had, so I am going to share the important details with you here.

Not only did I have wonderful parents raising me, but there was a whole wide world out there that I was, more or less, free to explore. I have a younger brother, Darryl, who's like a best friend to me to this day. And my older brother, Howard, to keep me out of the bad trouble and show me the right kind of trouble to get into! The world would soon become a Hollywood back studio lot for me. Trust me when I say that I perform all my own stunts.

Not just nuggets of wisdom from my childhood like when I learned jumping from moving vehicles and standing up to bullies, but also earning the respect of both my class as well as the instructors in US Army Ranger School too. I literally rocked and rolled between enlistments and then went on to crush it in the world of investment sales and sales management. I was a very successful stockbroker until I was quite literally Mr. Incredible-ed out of the major brokerage firm I worked for; I went independent after leaving. In the movie *The Incredibles*, Mr. Incredible gets reprimanded for helping a senior citizen save money on their portfolio without earning a commission for the company. He quits rather than trying to toe the line. Walking away from good money (actually, great) was hard! But once I was on my own, I was able to not only call my own shots but succeeded more than I ever did working for someone else. I'll cover the details shortly.

While I have arranged the chapters in chronological order, you'll note the chapters have subtitles that tell you exactly what each section is about, the action, or the lesson to be learned. Reading this book can be like learning from the actions of a big brother or close friend: take my mistakes as object lessons and be inspired to act through my successes. Take away what you want; it is more of an experiential toolbox than a self-help manual, though it is a bit of both, to be honest.

I have made sure to cherry-pick only those experiences and occasions that really stand out in my memory. But fear not, I've always endeavored to live a life less ordinary so this ought to be good!

Get comfy and look at the table of contents. I truly believe there's a chapter in here for everyone.

CHAPTER 1: "JUMP!"

Van Halen; 1983

Facing Fear, Trust, & Self-Assurance

Once I outlined this book and began working on it, one thing became clear to me. Modern storytellers all seem to be aware of something I learned quite a while ago: you are your own worst enemy, or more specifically, your fear is. Whether it is the Marvel Cinematic Universe and all the heroes at one point or another having to confront and control their fears, biographers show our favorite real-world heroes conquering what's holding them back (spoiler alert: it's fear). Nobody is working against you but you; nothing is holding you back but your own negative self-talk.

Sometimes you just need to take a leap of faith.

A disclaimer should forward this story: this took place in the early '80s when kids were still invincible; I'm kidding, but you *really* should take the concept from the following story, not the activity itself.

One day, I was hanging out with my older brother, Howard. I think he was fourteen at the time, putting me at about eleven years old. He and some of his buddies were going to go out and invited me to come along. It can be quite hard to express just how much a younger brother wants to be included in whatever the older one is doing; all I can say is it's pretty strong. There's hero worship and admiration there that can be as blinding as it is inspiring. He invited me along, but only under the condition that I must be "as tough" as they are; whatever they do, I have to do as well and be able to keep up.

Well, again, just like the bond between brothers, there was the universal law of boyhood to consider: any offer to demonstrate how "tough" you were had to be answered. This was long before any kind of softness was tolerated in a young man's culture. In the era of Stallone and Schwarzenegger, there were two things a boy could be: a tough guy or a sissy. Coupled with trying to impress my brother's friends, I was beside myself with excitement and overeager to prove myself worthy of the big kids' company. But what were they going to do?

Behind the house we were living in at the time was a forest with a river running through it. At most, it was ten feet deep and probably twenty feet wide. It was pretty deep for its width. Running over this river was a train bridge, the wooden trestle-type with no paths along the side.

We had started running toward this spot, the rest of them yelling, picking up the pace, laughing, and shouting, "We're gonna miss it!"

With a sinking feeling, I had an idea what they were looking to be on time for.

Sure enough, we get to the tracks just as the train comes around a curve. It's not moving too fast; the curve forced it to slow down.

Howard yells, "Hide!"

The oncoming train sent us scrambling down to the side and hunching down behind some bushes so the conductor couldn't see us as the train passed. Once it had gone by a little bit, Howard shouted again.

"Run!"

This sent us scrambling after the rear-most train car. I wasn't sure at first what we were running for until I saw one of his buddies grab the ladder attached to the side of the train car and hoist himself up. One by one, they grabbed on and pulled themselves on board.

Now, the train couldn't have been moving more than ten miles per hour. It was just creeping along, really, but it weighed hundreds of tons, and I was eleven. There's no stopping a train without slowing down first, so any misstep and you are losing a toe, foot, or leg, for sure. It was foolhardy, the whole thing. It was the kind of happy lark we pull as kids that makes our blood run cold thinking about it as adults. The whole hiding business was because the conductors really will call the cops on you. After all, they quite literally cannot stop. Some of those super-long, multi-engine trains, weighed down with coal or iron, take almost a full mile to slow down and stop! But we were dumb kids, as invincible as we were ignorant.

So I ran!

Tripping over my own feet, doing my best not to stumble over the wood ties, I ran as fast and as hard as I could. The rest of them had made it and were cheering me on. Legs pumping and a burgeoning young adult ego on the line, I gave it my all and reached the train with a huge jump. I am not sure what I thought they were going to do once everyone was on the train, but jumping right back off again was not what I had in mind.

Sure enough, the older kids ahead of me on the train began jumping off, sailing through the air and landing in the river.

My brother insisted "they did it all the time." To be honest, I was terrified, and I think my brother saw that once I got up on the train. Still, I had to jump at just the *exact* right moment, or I'd smack into the riverbank and break a leg or worse! I was too young to know that I would have to jump a little *before* my target, so my forward momentum would carry me as fast as the train was traveling. When it came time to jump, my brother yelled, "Jump!" And I jumped. It was absolutely a leap of faith indeed.

I clung on until the last possible second, and I remember my brother saying I *HAD* to jump when he said jump or else the train would take me all the way to China! Well, the rest of them were off already, and the train was speeding up! So at the exact moment I heard my brother yell at the top of his lungs, I left my fear on that train, and I JUMPED!

When my feet left the train car, it felt like I was going to crash into the nearside riverbank. But as we soared into the air, we demonstrated Newton's First Law and conserved our momentum, sailing forward and out over the water, landing precisely in the deepest point of the river.

We made it; we were alive!

Was it stupid? YES! It was stupid without a doubt. People can and sadly do die messing around with trains every year. To my eternal embarrassment, we would go on to do this again and again during the time we lived near the trestle, risking life and limb for fun and an adrenaline rush.

Not just fun, though, but a lesson I took with me and value still to this day.

No, not just profound respect for trains but a feeling that I could push through fear; if something was daunting or intimidating, it's possible to take it head-on and make it happen. When confronted with something challenging, it can be the hardest thing in the world to not charge into headlong, but when something is inevitable, it is best to anticipate it and deal with it as directly as possible.

Find an established place to cliff jump. Having been warned about the dangers of submerged hazards, though, maybe I should recommend finding a high dive someplace! It is excellent practice to note what you are afraid of and take steps to control or even undo that fear. You can't always rely on life offering you lessons; sometimes, you must go out of your way to find them. For instance, I would learn to get over a fear of confrontation by way of a bully named Ralph, but it was another lesson that, in hindsight, was truly not the right move in the first place!

You *should* find fears to push through, especially when you are young. The brain is still flexible in youth, the connections between thoughts and memories much more fluid than in adults. Break bad habits and create good ones; push through things you are afraid of and know you have no reason to be afraid. Being afraid of the dark is silly, but being afraid of a dark alley at 2:00 a.m. might be prudent. Don't be reckless or endanger yourself, of course, but find a controlled fright and take the plunge, like that literal plunge in my hometown. It was foolhardy and dangerous, yes, but it taught me to trust the experience of others, as well as my own abilities. The *grown-up* part of me wants to steer you toward a pool with a high dive, but the young crazy kid in me wants you to seek out that train trestle bridge over a river.

I think the second part of that story is relatively foundational to decisions I made later in life. The whole train-river-jump exercise—at least that first time we did it —was absolutely a team-building event. Adult me is a little embarrassed to admit we would go on to make that jump dozens of times. But while the rest of them had done it before, I had not. I took it on faith that they had done so and obviously lived through the experience. Putting my literal life in other people's hands would be something the military instills in its recruits, but it was not something I already knew at that time. Trust the recon; trust people (who have earned that trust), and you will have not only closer friendships, but you'll save yourself some misadventures too.

While I felt I had mastered the wilds behind my house, the bigger kids in junior high school would prove to be quite another matter.

Who would have thought that a future decorated member of the US Army Rangers was picked on and bullied as a kid? Well, most anyone whose memory of middle school was intact, I wager. If you managed to get through school without anyone ever singling you out for targeted abuse, you're a very lucky individual, indeed. More times than not, we suffer the random assault of a generally unpleasant idiot who spreads their bullying around evenly. Sometimes, however, there seems to be one particular jerk who will decide to target the same kid every chance they get.

I hope like hell you don't have anyone in your life that you need to direct this kind of lesson at. Maybe you are in middle school or high school and can use this advice directly. Perhaps it's just a different kind of bully—the browbeating, verbally abusive, condescending narcissists that never grew up because they never got popped in the jaw by a kid who was sick and tired of their BS. Whatever the case, sometimes overbearing personalities can only be deterred by a show of strength.

His name was Ralph. He was a little bit bigger than me at that age, which I was always self-conscious about. I wasn't used to being talked to the way he talked to me. It was my first actual conflict that I can recall that felt like it could end up in mortal combat. Okay, maybe not mortal combat, but a fistfight at minimum. He knew he was creating fear, as bullies do, and used it against me just as carefully as a surgeon with a scalpel. Or at least it felt like that at the time. But it felt a bit more like a nut punch than an operation: blunt and stupid. The kid was sucker punching me with words, and it kind of freaked me out and, quite frankly, REALLY pissed me off.

It was the oldest trick in the bully book: name-calling with a smug, evil grin. In hindsight, I now know that he called me every name in the book until he found the one that affected me the most. I barely even knew that "faggot" was derogatory when I was that age, but as a child of the '70s and '80s, I just knew it was "bad." It's not like I was even homophobic; it was a matter of childish bravado and uncontrollable temper more than anything. And the close talking, his persistence, and the tone he used. People had called me that before, but it never got under my skin.

I wound up bottling my rage until it blew. It wasn't until after losing my patience and my temper that I was able to push through my fear and really sock that little son of a biscuit right square in the mouth. I hit him so hard that it knocked him backward to the ground. I then proceeded to jump on top of him and kept on swinging! If you can picture the scene from *A Christmas Story* where Ralphie is on top of the bully spewing expletives, that is what happened with me. God, I love that scene.

Giving in to my rage like that led to my eternal embarrassment. I was never one for fighting outside of the occasional ass beating from my older brother, Howard. Walloping that kid is tough for me to admit, but it did make him leave me alone after that.

For that matter, no one ever screwed with me again. Junior high was the last time I was small, meek, and targeted for ridicule. By the end of high school, I had grown up and filled out a bit more. At the risk of being immodest, I was popular with the ladies too, which I only admit to illustrate how far I came in four years. Of course, this was also the era when playing guitar was considered cool, so what happened next probably had something to do with the popularity I gained by the time I graduated Apex High School in 1981.

The Ralph incident (which I like to refer to as "Sunday Bloody Sunday" even though it was on a Tuesday) taught me more than how to throw a punch. I learned that my fear was worse than what I was afraid of. He turned out to be nothing more than a little punk, loudmouthed and arrogant. He was nothing but an obnoxious jerk, and I had let him get the best of me. After I punched him, the fear he had filled me with for so long entered him, and I saw in his eyes the realization that he was no bigger than me, no better than me, and no better than anyone. In general, I've seen intimidation and the threat of force have the same effect.

You just can't let your fear show in a situation like that.

We're all afraid sometimes, but when the chips are down, you cannot let it paralyze you. At the same time, you can't allow it to cause you to do something stupid either. At some point in your life, you've probably seen dudes go through this elaborate ritual to avoid actual fighting: standing toe to toe, staring at each other, talking loud trash, and sometimes, literally, thumping chests? Just as in nature, challenges between members of the same species are almost always settled through non-violent displays and seldom deteriorate into actual fighting.

And for the record, of course, I got in trouble. So, before you go off just popping everyone in the mouth who pisses you off, you must know that unless you are in a ring with a ref or at least a few rules, fighting is going to have consequences, even if it's just bruises and a loss of respect from your friends and family. Because let's face it, folks, nobody respects a violent solution. Nobody ever proved a point with a fist beyond basic defense. Yes, there is no shortage of jerks in the world (and they seem to be multiplying, sadly), but unless they come in swinging at you directly, I promise it would be in your best interest to leave them be.

As the saying goes, some people are cruisin' for a bruisin', so even a pacifist should know how to pass a fist. Violence shouldn't be used to solve a problem, but neither should you just roll over and take it when someone is committing violence against you. I mean, come on. I enlisted into the

United States Army right out of high school. I know as well as anyone there is a time to make peace and a time to make war.

I do have to say that my dad was proud of me for standing up for myself. One evening at the dinner table, as I was complaining about Ralph, he looked over at me.

"Tell him that if he opens his mouth like that one more time, you'll put your fist down his throat!"

"So what do I do if he opens his mouth again?" I asked.

"You put your fist down his throat!" he stated, with no irony.

The truth is that this kind of scared me a little. Because now my own father had just taken away any reason for me to continue running from this sad excuse of a human being. I would now actually have to make a stand, and of course, as you know by now, that's precisely what I did.

Once all was said and done, I was punished, reprimanded by the school, and I think I was suspended for several days. Ha, well, truth be told, dad took me out for ice cream after school one day during that time, if memory serves me. School and the military both have the same kind of idea—fighting among yourselves is never allowed (outside of formal, refereed bouts, of course), and both parties will be punished no matter who started it. In this case, that was fine by me because while I did throw the first punch, it was

15

something I had to face. After all, while I didn't feel guilty, I knew I had messed up.

Going through a bit of tussle like that taught me a good deal about fear. That old chestnut "The only thing we have to fear is fear itself" rings as true today as it did when it was first spoken. While being afraid of a bully is one thing, how often do we hold back out of fear in life? Fear of the unknown, fear of change, fear of getting hurt. If we go through life avoiding pain at all costs, we go through life avoiding growth. Fear nothing if it is in the name of positive change. We expect growing pains in your legs and arms as kids get bigger, but mental growth can elicit just as much if not more pain than that.

By the time I jumped off the train and socked Ralph in the mouth (see what I did there?), I was quite confident. There was one undiscovered place of fear, though. A terror that grips the heart of every mortal and seldom lets us go.

I am talking about the fear of being in front of a crowd!

Almost universal, the feeling of having many eyes upon yourself is some people's worst nightmare. And while I was strangely attracted to being the center of attention, clammy palms and butterflies in my stomach froze my blood and stilled my feet. But I would eventually make a run at that phobia with the help of my friend, Tom Mauk, who had a shared love of music and was encouraging me to pursue my dreams of being on stage. Who would have thought that a skinny kid and a future army ranger and special operations soldier would be able to hold his own on stage in front of huge crowds as a guitar-playing rocker?

Now, I do have to rewind because it's not like I just picked up a six-string and began wailing like a boss. No, because I wanted to be a rock star like almost every boy in that era, but no one is born playing music. Unlike *every* boy in the period, I knew what it would take to become a rock star, and I was willing to do it. Kids either can't focus on anything longer than a few minutes, or they latch onto it and focus on nothing else! The rock band, KISS, who I worshiped to my dad's dismay, had demonstrated that having big hair and playing rock music so loud it makes your ears bleed was without a doubt a viable path to becoming a millionaire. And all the great bands of the '70s and '80s proved it could be wilder, louder, and faster too. I asked my dad for a guitar, and he looked at me silently for a minute before replying.

"I'll buy you a cheap guitar to learn on. If you learn to play it, I'll buy you a nice one."

For the uninitiated, a good, quality guitar is not a cheap purchase; as a performer, you typically invest in one high-quality guitar and then have a few cheaper ones for practice and, occasionally, smashing on stage like The Who. Just like anything, I suppose, there is a tremendous range in price and quality. So, he was okay thinking about buying me a nicer electric guitar like a Gibson SG, but only if I *actually* learned how to play first. With all the excitement of a kid on Christmas, I ran right to my copy of *Spiderman* and flipped to the back where The US School of Music course regularly had advertisements, and I clipped out the order form to purchase a complete course on beginners' guitar.

They also sold cheap—I mean, *really* cheap—acoustic guitars to learn on.

Perfect! Everything I needed in one place to start down the path to rock 'n' roll greatness. Back then, I think the entire cost was like $39.95. Ha! That, of course, was a large sum of money in the '70s for a young boy, but somehow, between my allowance and earning extra money working for my dad, I got it done!

I remember the day the package arrived. It was the cheapest and quite possibly the crappiest acoustic six-string on planet earth, but it was all mine, and I loved it! Well, I loved it enough to learn on it anyway. The rickety thing barely held a tune, snapped strings like floss, and made my fingers bleed. But I got my basic fretwork down and mastered a few chords. I'd practice for hours to the complete irritation of my family and going through chords and fumbling my way through songs until I got them down.

The first song I ever learned to play was "Love Me Tender" by Elvis Presley. It was that song that convinced my dad to buy me a nicer guitar. While I wouldn't actually rock out on stage for many years, it got to the point where I felt good enough with my mic and amp that I would set up in our garage and make it look as if I was on stage. By the time I graduated, I had played in a couple of small bands, nothing of any significance, just more about jamming and having fun. We never played any big shows, just friends and the occasional few nosy strangers. But it cemented what I had suspected: there was a part of me that had a taste and a burning desire to be in front of a crowd. A little corner of my brain now *knew* that I had the skills to be a rocker and performer, and I would grow up considering it a viable career option.

Listen to me, please: You must step it up in life. Literally, take a step toward the mic and perform in front of people or take steps toward even the most daunting of goals. I live by a simple rule: regardless of how many people you get in front of, one or one thousand, *ALWAYS* leave them better off than you found them.

Did you know that most people surveyed say they would rather die than speak in front of an audience? Even just a half-dozen people can make your heart feel like it's going to seize up and stop beating or fly right out of your chest. It can be hard enough for some folks to go to class or work and interact with people all the time. Well, try adding standing on an elevated stage facing an audience with all eyes on you and with amplification and spotlights! The fear of failure compounds. But all of a sudden, there you are. YOU are, for real, the life of the party, and knowing if you fail, the party is going to be lame. I encourage you to face your fears head-on. You don't have to be a rock star standing on a stage, but I firmly believe we're ALL rock stars in our own way. If you keep reading, I intend to prove it!

I'll finish with this thought: By the time I graduated from high school, I had gotten over many hang-ups that, in my opinion, hold so many people back. Wanting to put my newfound courage and skills to the greatest good and confident in my ability to overcome any obstacle, it was with a great deal of excitement that I enlisted in the US Army as soon I graduated. I entered the army on September 1, 1981, when I was only seventeen years old. Yep, I needed parental consent, which I'm pretty sure my dad had no problem giving! I remember the day they dropped me off at the MEPS (Military Entrance Processing Station) and my mom's words.

"I won't have time to miss you because, with that mouth of yours, they'll ship your butt back home in no time!"

Aaaand there you have it!

Take the leap, stand up to the bully, and be ready to WORK for your dreams.

CHAPTER 2: "LEARN TO FLY"

Foo Fighters, 1999

Maintain High Standards; Ignore the Haters

We moved to Tampa when I was in the middle of high school, but we bounced back to North Carolina my senior year; the credit systems were different, but in my favor, so I wound up only needing to go to school part-time! This allowed me to go to school from 8:00 a.m. leave by noon. I had a job at the local mall so I could work to earn a small paycheck and have time to get my homework done. My mom had enrolled me in kindergarten a year early, and I was born in September. Therefore, when I graduated, I was only seventeen years old. Nowadays, modern school systems will encourage kids born in the fall like this to wait a year; maybe being the youngest in all my classes forever set me up for getting used to working extra hard.

In case you haven't noticed by now, I'm one of the infuriating people who follow orders to the T, and I carry through with consistency. The army made their expectations crystal clear right from day one: a well-made clean bunk, a pressed neat uniform, and an otherwise formal military attire and attitude when mustered or training. There is just a part of myself that picks things up quickly, but it's not through any natural knack or gift—just the hard work, discipline, and maybe knowledge of what it takes to pick up a new skill. In this case, the skill was to be a soldier.

21

Those of us who grew up in this era remember the jingle: "Be All That You Can Be." It wasn't long before the drills singled me as a good example. I became a squad leader, which irritated many of the guys in my platoon because I was only seventeen years old when I started basic training. It would last a total of thirteen weeks. Yes, longer than the traditional eight weeks of basic that many are used to or have been told about. I was in the infantry; it was technically called OSUT (One Station Unit Training). This consisted of eight weeks of "basic" training and five weeks of infantry training. After completion, I headed straight to three weeks of US Army Airborne School. All my training was conducted at Fort Benning, Georgia: home of the infantry.

Well, the rest of my squad got a little tired of me being the top soldier all the time and plotted a little revenge. One morning, I was grabbed by several soldiers in my platoon right before a muster formation; that's the scene in movies where they blow the horn and everyone runs up and falls into formation, gets inspected, screamed at, and generally starts the day with the drill sergeant's voice ringing in their ears. I was standing tall and looking sharp as usual, heading toward the formation. Being the first squad leader, I'm the point man that the rest of the platoon lines up on, so I had to be there first. From out of nowhere, a small group of my fellow soldiers waylaid me.

They grasped me by the arms, hauled me back into the barracks, and threw me into the shower, soaking me to the bone, then ran off to the formation so as not to be late. I still made it on time, but I was soaking wet: dripping water, boots squelching, and my pressed and starched uniform sodden. Suffice to say, my uniform, hair, and general comportment were not up to standard. The drill sergeants seemingly ganged up and had a great time screaming and shouting an inch from my face, demanding why the normally well-put-together infantry soldier was standing in the ranks looking like a wet dog.

As loud and as close to my face as he got, I never said a word about how I ended up in my current condition. This, of course, just pissed the drills off even more! They decided to send me to the sawdust pit (where hand-to-hand combat is practiced and physical training is conducted), and I was instructed to low-crawl through the pit for two hours. This is precisely what it sounds like: slinging my M16 rifle across my back and dragging a thirty-five-pound rucksack. I spent 120 minutes squirming through a vast field of sawdust. The entire time, different drills were taking turns yelling at me to turn in the guilty. If I did, then the torture would stop.

Well, I never did reveal who did what, and they eventually let me out of the pit, and I went on with the day's training in my sawdust-covered BDUs. As it turns out, I had managed to earn the respect of my platoon *and* earn the respect of the leadership. They used me as an example one more time, pointing out how I remained loyal to the company and my peers under all circumstances.

I have my suspicions. I can readily imagine some of the drills putting a few of my "buddies" (I use the word buddy loosely) up to it to see how I'd react. One drill sergeant in particular, Drill Sergeant Mears, couldn't stand me. He rode my ass every single day! If I had ratted any one of them out, no doubt I would have "failed." I've worked with a lot of people who are all professional and neat as a pin but completely fall to pieces when the unexpected happens or are quick to place blame: neither are helpful in emerging situations. Even if it was a simple prank concocted by irritated and jealous peers, I knew I had to handle it with dignity. After all, I absolutely knew that the army expects nothing but the best in an infantry soldier. It wasn't long before I was distinguishing myself in even more significant ways.

Every step you take in the military, if you exceed your leaders' expectations, they can offer you more opportunities than the "average" soldier is ever afforded. For example, applying for Special Forces or becoming a ranger. As you might expect of me by now, my curiosity and thrill-seeking spirit would rule the day and faster than expected. I entered basic training as a Private (E-1), and within eighteen months, while assigned to the 1/505th Airborne Infantry, 82d Airborne Division, I was promoted to Sergeant E5. To let you know what kind of accomplishment this was, the time-in-service requirement at the time was three years, meaning you could *not* be promoted to a sergeant until you had served three full years in the army. So many people told me that it couldn't be done! Well, I have never in my life bought into that, and you shouldn't either. Anything you set your mind to *can* be accomplished, and the rules are absolutely meant to be broken!

All told, my first enlistment was four years, from September 1981 to July of 1985, and would take me from basic training and jump school in Fort Benning, Georgia, to my first combat operation in Grenada and back again. Boot camp had kicked my ass, both literally and figuratively. Little did I know, basic training would turn out to be a cakewalk compared to the training I would undertake in my future. As expected, however, upward mobility in the army requires blood, sweat, and tears in a genuine way. Tears are acceptable, but no sobbing; you don't want to jam those emotions down until they rot, but neither do you want them running away with you. In any case, I was thankful for the experiences in my service to my country. I am a patriot for sure and always will be.

Before we move on, have you ever wondered what airborne school I like? I mean, why would anyone jump from a perfectly good aircraft in flight, right?

Ground Week
The first week is called ground week for a few reasons, not least of which is that we were still "grounded," with no actual parachute jumps allowed until you learn the basics. It doesn't matter if you've gone skydiving before; there are bad habits to unlearn, and you need to know how to jump as part of a battalion, in any case. They teach you all kinds of fun stuff, like how to hit the ground without breaking your ankles. They also go over the basics of the round T-10

style and the rectangular T-11 parachutes. We spent days learning how to fall, exit the craft in a group, strap on the gear, safety check, and maintain the gear.

You'd think falling is easy, but when the Black Hats (instructors wearing black ball caps) are walking around making sure you are doing it right, it becomes advanced chess. There is a "right way to fall," and I took to it quick. It's called a PLF (Parachute Landing Fall), distributing the forces of impact along your legs and upper body so you don't fracture, dislodge, or sprain anything. Parachuting, you hit the ground between ten and fifteen miles per hour, the equivalent of hopping off a nine-to-twelve-foot wall. We jumped off platforms about that height into sand, gravel, and all sorts of surfaces to prepare for different drop zones. The week ended with dropping off zip lines and a thirty-four-foot platform that put our new skills to the ultimate crash test.

You can't get to week two without passing all the jump training tests *and* the standard army PT test for seventeen-to-twenty-one-year-olds, regardless of age and how long ago you passed it the first time. As you might expect, this week has the most significant number of washouts, and you are either cut orders for worldwide assignments or, rarely, recycled to some earlier classes to try again.

Tower Week
By week two, they had us parachuting, but not from a plane. There's a four-armed, 250-foot tower they drop us from, if we don't lose our lunch on the tower and swing

ladders first. We practice rushing out of a mock thirty-four-foot-tall aircraft door as a group and the all-important parachute malfunction solution drills. Modern parachutes have a smaller backup reserve chute in case of malfunctions, so we had to go through the motions where we cut away the first and deploy the reserve, which always puts the fear of God into us.

Drilling new actions, repeating them until you can literally do them blindfolded, forced that action into your brain's reflex memory. You become able to do them without thinking, so when the inevitable crisis hits, you are only thinking about what you absolutely need to do. Fighters train to perform blocks and strikes into near-automatic responses. Musicians practice for hours a day, so the chords get conditioned into their hands. Soldiers drill every action from waking to sleeping, so we can think about tactics and battlefield awareness instead of where our bullets are or if our boots are tied when the enemy drops in. No amount of training and practice is ever wasted.

We used the T-10 type parachute that's technically not steerable. You'd have to manipulate the risers in order to turn the chute or to "slip" away from a fellow jumper in the air. It's not an easy task, and I found myself grunting a LOT when attempting to maneuver this beast. There's more washing out from this week as people discover REAL quick if they have what it takes. It's one thing to jump from military-grade playground equipment and quite another to get dangled in the air and dropped two-hundred and fifty feet. Assuming you get the hang of all of that, you go onto week three: Jump Week.

Jump Week
This is where it all comes together. Piling into a C-130 (turboprop) or C-17 (jet turbine), which are both immense four-engine cargo planes, we took off from Lawson Army Airfield, and it was barely any time at all before we were over Fryar Field, the training drop zone. We lined up, but as loud as the aircraft was with the doors open, wind rushing, and prop engines screaming, I swear you could hear a pin drop; all eyes fixed on a glowing red light next to the opened doors. The pilot lowered the plane down to jump speed, and the crew did pre-jump checks. Typically, we hit three thousand feet, which was the jump altitude for practice jumps. Combat altitude was eight hundred feet. The plane moved along with a cruising speed of about 113 knots before we exited the aircraft. Once the crew had made sure they did all they could to ensure we didn't "burn-in," the green light lit up, and we did the "airborne shuffle" out the door.

We all file out, jumping until the green light turns red, then we stop, the pilot circles back around and passes over the LZ again. The green light flicks back on, and more of us jump out. The process repeats until everyone makes the jump. During jump week, they had us make jumps fully combat-ready with all our gear, and we did a couple of so-called *Hollywood jumps* too. To graduate from jump school, you must complete five successful jumps, including at least one night jump.

Suffice to say, I graduated with "flying" colors, once again exemplifying the kind of attention to detail and tireless work ethic that got me thrown in the shower in basic training.

My first combat experience.

This is one of those little-big military operations not many people remember, let alone know about. It only lasted a few days on the books, though I was in the country for several weeks. The whole thing was largely overshadowed in the media by the bombing of a US Marine barracks in Beirut just two days before. A terrible tragedy to say the least.

A tiny synopsis: After gaining independence from the UK in 1974, a communist group called the New Jewel Movement had seized power in 1979. They suspended the constitution and took a few political prisoners. You know, the real fun guys. The inevitable power struggles of the new government led to the leader being put under house arrest in 1983 by his own cabinet for not sharing power as they had agreed to. His supporters got ornery, mobbed up, sprung him, and the two sides eventually clashed. Almost two dozen soldiers, civilians, cabinet members, and union leaders died.

The US received a formal appeal for intervention from the Organization of Eastern Caribbean States and a secret plea from the Governor-General Scoon of Grenada. Still, he wouldn't officially sign the declaration asking for help until a day or two later.

Our strike force was made up of the Seventy-Fifth Rangers, the army's rapid deployment force, Marines, Delta Force, SEALs, us, and more, totaling about 7,600 troops, joined by the Jamaican military forces and units from the RSS (Regional Security System). RSS is another Caribbean conglomerate of islands that signed on for mutual aid and defense. In any case, this was not a popular operation beyond the islands themselves.

No one was really worried about the Grenada Army itself, as it lacked any kind of air defenses and was vastly outnumbered. No, we were on the lookout for Cuba and whether they'd send in support. It would turn out to be Cuban nationals living in Grenada that would give us a more complex operational theater than anticipated, which is military-speak for "things got hairy." You see, Castro had this whole "citizen-soldier" thing where if you were a citizen of Cuba, you were required to take a few months of military training once you were of age. So there was unexpected resistance the whole way, not just the usual bases and strongholds but villages and even the open countryside.

After all was said and done, the UK publicly supported us, but I guess Thatcher gave us the third degree in secret. The rest of the world basically looked at it like American aggression again, completely ignoring that we were there by invitation only and left as soon as we could. Looking it up now, the UN General Assembly voted it "a flagrant violation of international law" by a vote of 108 to nine! Well, the whole world might not have approved. Still,

Grenada herself made the day a national holiday called Thanksgiving, commemorating the freeing of political prisoners who were subsequently elected to office, so it was for a great reason.

I served my tour and made sure the jump wings sewn on my chest weren't just a decoration. That first day, after the Seventy-Fifth Rangers captured Pointe Salines International Airport, we came in with land reinforcements, secured the airport's perimeter, and took surrenders, including a hangar full of almost one hundred troops.

All told, I think there were close to twenty casualties on our side, a few totaled Huey's, and a whole lot of injured soldiers. It was an invasion and pitched battle. Make no mistake. We completed the mission. I got my taste of action, but when all was said and done, I didn't reenlist in the army. Not right away, at least. I was happy with my military career; I was just ready to get out from under the command structure and do my own thing. As it turned out, I would make a career change that goes a little beyond "lateral" and all the way to "drastic."

As soon as I got out, I had to deal with some family stuff, a little distraction that tied me up but gave me time to reflect on what I wanted to do. I mean, I had thought about going back into music, but being back home really drove to heart what I really wanted. Being back home, reflecting on growing up, my training, and my tour of duty, I was drawn to the same thing again and again. As at odds as it seemed, I knew what path I wanted the next stage of my life to take.

It turned out what I really wanted was to rock and roll!

CHAPTER 3: "THE BOYS ARE BACK IN TOWN"

Thin Lizzy, 1978

Go for Your Dreams; Seek the Stage

I got out of the army in 1985; living in Cary, North Carolina, it was peaceful stillness compared to active duty, in spite of the family wrinkles we were ironing out.

With a burning desire to rock, I had a few hundred bucks in my pocket and, after talking to a buddy of mine living in Fort Lauderdale, decided Florida was as famous for its nightlife as any other big city.

Jumping into my Malibu Classic, I hit I-95 South and never looked back. Well, I mean, I reflect on the past all the time, so maybe I should say, "hit the road with no regrets." You must look back, or you risk not learning from your mistakes; as long as you consider the past, learn from your missteps, and always look for ways to improve, every mistake is a learning opportunity.

Everyone makes mistakes, but you only have to make them once.

As cliché as it sounds, it was with my head full of dreams and the highway unwinding before me that I drove toward my future with a wide-eyed intensity. I hadn't felt this way

33

since the first time I jumped from an aircraft in fright, er—I mean flight!

My buddy, Tom Mauk, who I served with in the 82d Airborne Division, called me up one day not long after we got out and said, "Hey, I'm down here in Fort Lauderdale. I love it down here, and you know why!"
Okay, so there's a little backstory here about Fort Lauderdale, if you'll let me digress for just a moment.

I think it was the second year we were in the army that Tom suggested we put in for leave during spring break and head down to Fort Lauderdale. This was back in 1982 when spring break in Florida was still completely off the chain! I'm talking complete debauchery and hedonism. Everyone was covered in beer and tequila, wet T-shirt contests everywhere you looked, Jell-O shots, live music, and straight-up dancing (and vomiting; sorry, just keeping it real.) in the streets! We got our seven-day leave approved, hopped in my Honda Accord Coupe, and hit I-95 south right out of Fayetteville, NC.

The problem was that once we arrived in Fort Lauderdale, we didn't have the foresight to reserve a hotel room ahead of time. Remember, this was in the early '80s: no iPhones, no internet, no Airbnb—you get the point. We ended up living in my incredibly small Honda Accord Coupe in the parking lot of a public beach. Believe it or not, the police had no problem with this. It turned out a lot of spring break goers were in the same boat, and we made lots of friends from our parking lot hotel.

Anyway, Tom had called me and said he loved it down there, and he had this job and was all set up and stuff.

"Why don't you come down and check it out?"

I met Tom in basic training; we not only went through jump school together but were assigned to the same battalion and platoon at Fort Bragg, which is rare. We even served in Grenada together, which was our first combat operation. One of my really clear memories of serving in Grenada was the day we were on a recon mission with a Grenadian guide. The concern was that our guide, although vetted, possibly could have been part of the PRA (People's Revolutionary Army). These were Grenadian citizens who had agreed to work with the Russian soldiers to complete the airport needed to fly in large aircraft carrying Soviet weaponry.

Tom and I were on this recon, and after hours of moving through the jungle and up a small mountain, we stopped for a short break. We found this tree on its side lodged in between two other trees, forming a makeshift bench. The mountainside was so steep that we could sit on the log and lean back against the ground like we were in a recliner. At first, we talked about what type of evasive action we'd take if our guide was, in fact, leading us into an ambush, but oddly, that conversation quickly changed into a discussion on just how awesome a PB&J and a glass of milk would taste right about that moment!

It's weird: even though you know you could be facing possible death, your mind will always find a way to give you some peace. At least, that's what I believe. I did face more potential life or death situations after this point, so for me, this was always the case which I'm thankful to God for.

Tom, as I said, was living in Fort Lauderdale at the time, and I decided Florida was as good of a place as any to do what I wanted to do and took him up on the offer. We'd always stayed in touch; truthfully, it hadn't been *that* long since we left the army. We had always gotten along well, and it was great to go from living in the barracks to an apartment with a roommate I already knew.

The transition from active duty to civilian life can be jarring, not least of which because you go from being a part of a well-oiled, disciplined machine of hundreds of people to just you. Having my roommate be not only someone I served with, but a real friend, was great. Having someone to pal around with who went through exactly what I went through really helped me shift gears gradually, ease out of the army headspace, and focus on what I really wanted.

I knew that if I were going to get into a band, it would have to be a place that had a booming nightlife, and remember, I had been to Fort Lauderdale on spring break: the live band scene was huge! For context, in the '80s, Fort Lauderdale was like spring break all the time. Kind of like how New Orleans almost has that Mardi Gras flavor going on year-round. Both of these destinations have done what they can to stem the flow of drunken idiots into their cities nowadays, but in the mid-'80s, it seemed like there was never enough.

At any rate, I only crashed on Tom's couch for a few weeks and eventually got a job working in a factory at Peter Powell Stunt Kites. Not only did I make the kites, but I would sell and teach people how to fly them on the beach. These are those two-handled nylon kites that you can steer and do tricks with. I spent my days with the kites while I hit the bulletin boards and clubs at night looking around for anyone who needed a guitarist for a band.

I wound up finding a rockabilly band that was just forming up, and I was part of its creation. We called ourselves Convertible Ken and the Ragtops. It was a good group of fellas: Steve, Chris, Dave, and me. We believed in big guitars and even bigger hair! I'm saying we kept the hair spray brand Aqua Net in business! Although not my first choice, I had always liked rockabilly artists like Carl Perkins, Elvis Presley, Johnny Burnette, and Jerry Lee Lewis. If those don't ring a bell, then surely, you've heard of the Stray Cats. As a band, we grooved together well and had a great stage show.

We stayed with the rockabilly gig for a while but ultimately left Fort Lauderdale, headed across alligator alley, and ended up in Fort Myers, where Steve, Chris, and Dave were originally from. It was nice having a little help from family when we needed a hand. In a new town, I had little besides practice. Once in Fort Myers, we were picked up by a management company, and we completely revamped ourselves. We went from a four-piece rockabilly band named Convertible Ken and the Ragtops to The Unknown, a five-piece, full-fledged rock 'n' roll band.

On a typical night, we'd open with "Born to Be Wild" by Steppenwolf. We started every third set with "Ain't That a Shame" by Cheap Trick, but we'd perform the live version from the album "Live at Budokan" because it had this long cool intro, and we would choreograph our moves on stage. The most requested song, and one of my favorites to play as it has this cool dual lead part that Dave, our lead guitarist, and I played, was "The Boys Are Back in Town" by Thin Lizzy.

Mind you, I wasn't then, nor have I ever been, the best guitar player, but I didn't suck by any measure, either. I also wasn't the lead singer. That was Steve Ballard because he had the voice of an angel and could really, I mean, *really* sing! Though, I did do lead on some songs to help Steve give his voice a break. I mean, we played four sets a night that lasted forty to fifty minutes in length, and we did this on average five to six nights a week. I would sing for songs like "Shakin'" by Eddie Money, "Love Removal Machine" and "Wildflower" by The Cult, as well as "I Will Follow" by U2. I think there were a few more; otherwise, I sang backup and harmony and played rhythm guitar. I LOVED every single night being up on that stage with those guys.

Chris and I lived on a sailboat for a little while there. His father managed a nice marina right before you crossed the intercoastal into Fort Myers Beach, which gave us a cheap place to live while we got our act together. It was a bit cramped and could get a bit smelly, but it gave us a place to get our footing, and of course, that proximity in a cramped small sailboat would be a torture test of our personalities. If we could mesh living on a boat and living on the road together without driving each other nuts, then that was a great accomplishment. However, our time on the ship would be cut short when a hurricane came through and sunk the damn thing! Man, I loved living on that boat.

When we were on the road, we had a sound guy named Dano. He was retired and living in Cape Coral, Florida, at the time. Dano had been the sound engineer for the mega '70s rock band, Foghat, back in the day and helped us get our live sound dialed in.

Dano came to see us play one night at a club called Serena's and was like, "Man, you guys sound terrible; I mean, you're good as a band, but your sound is really crappy." He offered to improve our sound for a relatively small paycheck, and you know what? It really helped! As long as we were touring Florida, he was our sound man and took care of us as well as his wife. He made sure the sound was mixed perfectly, and any effects that were needed in our songs were put in on cue.

It would have been easy to blow him off. We were a bunch of young big-haired rockers with the typical rock and roll attitude. Distortion and noise were still cool, and as rockers, we weren't beholden to the same musical fidelity standards as other, more mainstream acts. But we were always open

39

to suggestions and constructive criticism, so we took it without hesitation. We had an opportunity for growth.

Our sound was incredible now; we'd play four to five hours almost every night, and we were up gigging five to six nights per week—paying gigs, of course. I was a working musician, and whenever we played, we got *paid*. We put in the work, as well, practiced as much as we could, and self-promoted like our lives depended on it. Work hard, play hard was our motto. We were living the dream—the first step to superstardom. The Unknown got a little well-known, toured quite a bit, made a bunch of demos, and spread them around to every label, radio station, and promoter we could get in front of. We were going for it: looking for a popular breakthrough and trying to get that record deal. We were going to be rock stars, dammit! I mean, we *were* rock stars, but we wanted to be national, worldwide. These were indeed the best days of my life, or so I thought.

After a few years, by 1988, I decided the rocker's life just wasn't for me. I mean, you can well imagine: the '80s were quite famous for rockers overdosing and publicly embarrassing themselves. Sadly, many of them died from drugs. The truth is that I had been doing cocaine for quite a while, and I had convinced myself that I was only doing it for "medicinal" purposes. By that, I mean a typical day for me was waking up around noon and cracking a beer. Then, depending on where we were playing, I'd go lay on a beach somewhere nearby, and, of course, we always played at bars, there as well. I'd drink most of the afternoon and then get ready to go to the club early for any rehearsals. Of course, once in the club, you can imagine I'd have a drink, and they honestly just kept coming for the rest of the night. Not to mention, have you ever gone to see a live band play? Ever buy them a drink or a shot? That happened EVERY night!

To combat the drinking that ultimately makes you tired, I started doing lines of coke. It wakes you up and makes you feel invincible, but as fantastic as that may sound, the fact of the matter is while you think you sound great, chances are you sound like shit, and you start acting like it as well.

Sadly, when we were doing a photo shoot and setting up our main promotional band photo, I was so hungover that they had to set me on a stool. The pic ultimately came out looking great, but it wasn't what we had intended. I woke up one day with blood coming from my nose quite profusely and decided then and there that if I didn't give up this lifestyle, I'd wake up dead one day. That's dark humor, but the fact is that many don't wake up. I guess I was just aware of how destructive it all was and knew I didn't want what came along with rock stardom.

I know it's possible to rock without being loaded. There's absolutely no reason we couldn't have continued doing what we were doing with me sober; it happens all the time. As well as all of the other things that went along with it too: the long nights, irregular schedule, and constant chaos. Some people thrive in a state of perpetual upheaval, but I do require a certain amount of predictability.

41

Now, I knew I still wanted to be a rock star, but maybe I wasn't sure of the vehicle; the focus of a crowd, directing or even creating the energy shared by a large group, was fantastic, and I was good at it. I didn't just want to tour around, work crazy hours, blow my eardrums out, and get hammered every night anymore. Unfortunately, at the time of writing this, I have terrible tinnitus. A constant never-ending ringing in my ears which many people suffer from. I have no doubt it's from a combination of my army days and my band days, but I can honestly tell you, I wouldn't change a single thing.

I enjoyed my time in the military and still had this desire to be, well, a badass. There, I admitted it. I truly wanted to be a rock star *and* a badass! I was still young at twenty-seven, so I decided to reenlist in the US Army, and this time, I would go all in and sign up under a ranger contract. It might seem a bit strange to go from the world of rock and roll to being back into the army, but the rangers, and eventually Delta Force, are as close to rock stars as the military got back then. While I had gotten used to the freedom of a working, touring musician, I knew that Rangers' entire gig was more free form than standard infantry movements.

Rangers Lead the Way, as the motto says.

So, I went.

CHAPTER 4: "RIGHT NOW!"

Van Halen; 1991

Tenacity; Determination; Never Lose Your Cool

It was 1988, and my thirst for personal badassdom led me back to military life. Having achieved the highest point of being a rocker, I wanted to see what heights I could get to in the army. It was the mid-'80s, and the pinnacle of human potential was still Rambo and Schwarzenegger. This isn't to give credit to pop culture for inspiring me to reenlist, but I think most young men in those days dreamed of being a badass like in the stars in the movies. Tired of rocking and needing to roll, I signed up for a guaranteed Airborne ranger contract. (This was provided I succeeded in the training. If you fail, then you are put up for worldwide assignment.)

There would be many times I wanted to quit. There were times I felt like I was going to die. But you just put one foot in front of the other and keep going regardless of how many times you say to yourself that you're going to quit. Some people talk about taking on hardships one day at a time, but sometimes you just have to think about it *one minute at a time*. Focus on the task at hand, then the next useful thing. Hell, even Elsa in *Frozen 2* mentions just doing "the next good thing" when you don't know what else to do, which makes sense. Once you conquer fear, the next step can be crucial. But giving up and quitting is not an option.

Ranger School is a leadership school, although many folks think it's only a combat operations school. The course teaches tactics and taking charge of a squad—not just warcraft, but leading and inspiring men to accomplish a mission: a ranger patrol. Would-be students get three weeks of the Ranger Indoctrination Program, then you have to go through three more weeks of the pre-ranger course, and from there, provided you haven't already failed or washed out, you go right into Ranger School itself. There was a prescreen in place because it is a brutally challenging course, and only the best of the best can attend. When I started, my course was the very first seventy-two-day program ever run. Historically, our nine-week course was only fifty-eight days long, but it was expanded, supposedly for desert training. I'm sure some one-star general decided that it needed to be more challenging than it already was. This made our class's attrition numbers super high with a 72 percent washout rate. There were about four hundred men when we started, and by the time we made it to graduation, only about 120 of us were left standing and graduated.

As I said earlier, it's a brutal course. I was already assigned to the Seventy-Fifth Ranger Regiment and the RIP (Ranger Indoctrination Program) detachment, where I served for several years. My younger brother, Darryl Paulk, came through the RIP detachment while I was working there and would go on to serve in the Second Ranger Battalion out of Fort Lewis, Washington. The Second Ranger Battalion was affectionately referred to as The Killer Battalion, and he'd serve with them for many years. Like I said, though, US

Army Ranger School is a leadership school. And although it's a volunteer course and as grueling as it is, some ranger students have died going through the system. It's truly something that can't be explained; only those that have earned the coveted Ranger Tab understand.

It's important to note that a soldier's rank is never displayed, nor is a soldier addressed by their rank while attending Ranger School. So, people don't have insignia on their collar or sleeve, meaning it doesn't matter if you're a full bird colonel or a specialist; since no rank insignia are worn, everyone is treated the same. (Like crap, basically!) This surprises some people until you realize that there's no better way to instill excellent leadership skills in everyday life than hiding the bosses among the population. If you want to see a condescending "leader" shape up really quick, you take away their rank (position) and put them in a situation where they must EARN their peers' respect.

There are always people that kiss ass, or even just over-achieve when the boss is around, but start acting like God's gift and not lifting a finger when they leave. This nips those kinds of problems right in the bud, and you better believe it was satisfying to watch a few of these so-called "leaders" squirm, not knowing whose ass to kiss and who's to bite. In the wild, a wolf pack isn't ruled with unbending authority by a single, aggressive male but by a mated pair who lead according to the benefit of everyone. There's no so-called "omega wolf," either; the myth of the necessary underdog or beloved lackey is garbage. There's never a benefit to singling one person out and using them as the group's

45

bastard. If there's one person in your group everyone rags on, or even just makes do small things, knock it off. That is, as folks say, toxic. Any wolf dominating the rest and taking more than their fair share gets run out of the pack. "Army Of One" is all fine and well, but we are always training toward operating as a team.

The squad and tactics training is divided up into phases that are mostly centered around different terrains, geography, and temperate climates. Phases build on each other. You are forced to learn basic, intermediate, and even advanced skills while patrolling, moving overland, and engaging with simulated enemy fire, while under minimal food rations, always sleep-deprived, and exerting constant extreme physical effort. Everything you can think of that might simulate an incursion into enemy territory or add to the difficulty is done. The imagination used to test Rangers is nothing short of boundless.

There's an emphasis on training against live targets too. Most mission ops are of the so-called war-game type, which, believe me, is more war and less game. There's an opposing force, enemy-controlled territory, and even a plot. There's this whole story they create to give the encounters as much of a real-world context as possible. When I went through the course, we were simulating the takedown of a drug-funded terrorist cartel. Officially known as OPFOR scenarios, we trained against a live opposing force. They are real soldiers, usually on TDY (temporary duty), who are trained specifically for the task. While traditionally called war games, military training might be a lot of things, but it's no game.

Benning Phase

Training in the army is segmented, building on itself but never afraid to go back and drill the basics. Remember, the more you do something, the less you have to think about it. Ranger School is equal parts dizzying instruction of new knowledge and crushing repetition of practice. Held in Camp Rogers at Ft. Benning, Georgia, this is your general-purpose butt-whooping program: run five miles in forty minutes over rolling terrain, rudimentary water combat, day/night land navigation, a little demolition, and more push-ups, sit-ups, and chin-ups than you can stomach. Some of us really do push ourselves so hard we lose our lunch, and in some of the near-starvation scenarios we are put through, that would be a disaster indeed.

The land navigation section introduces the idea of "light discipline." A small red flashlight is given to you for map reading only, and you use it to find your way across the terrain and get booted. Use a red light outdoors or anywhere you don't want to ruin your night vision. Red light doesn't mess with your eye's natural night vision, so you don't get dazzled or get those temporary floaty spots. It is amazing how well you can see on a moonless night if your night vision is intact. We call it "lumes," which is slang for luminosity or luminous.

The emphasis this week is on squad combat operations as well. We are learning to think and work as a platoon, understanding how to work as a unit—the ultimate team-building experience. In fact, it was normal for CEOs to lead their middle managers up to a mock-army camp and send everyone through a version of boot just for this type of experience back in the '80s and '90s. Nothing solidifies a working team like a shared ordeal, a close-working relationship forged in fire. If the organizer realizes the purpose is for team building, not actual combat training, these activities can work on civilians. We train for months as part of a military career; those corporate retreats last a weekend and mean to instill more efficient paper-pushing and managing employees more strategically. While going through a stressful situation and overcoming it will bond you tighter than anything, if the leader is seen as incompetent or needlessly strict, the only cohesion you will be inspiring is mutiny!

Mountain Phase

The second phase takes place in Camp Frank D. Merrill in the mountains near Dahlonega, Georgia. Here, we learned how to operate in a mountainous environment. In addition to intermediate combat operations, at this time, we were taught military mountaineering, climbing, rappelling, and how to patrol in extremely uneven terrain when visibility can sometimes be nil. Surviving in extreme weather conditions, the fundamentals of raids, ambushes, and reconnaissance are also learned now.

This phase is the first time working at elevation for a lot of people, the thin air making every action an effort. Your body's metabolism must adjust, but everything is pretty normal once you do—beyond the wind, crazy weather, blizzards, and cold, that is. This is also the phase where they really stress the hell out of an individual's stamina. Lack of sleep, extremely minimal food (an average of one MRE a day), and regular hard labor are all ratcheted up, pushing us as far as we can and further. Sticking us on a mountain when doing all this adds to the stress by design. The careful piling on is a key part of training but sadly washed many men out of the course.

In the mountain phase is where I lost my ranger buddy, Adam Such. No, not to death. I'll explain.

This is going to sound a bit odd, but bear with me. When you start Ranger School, everyone is assigned a ranger buddy. You are to go nowhere without your buddy, and I mean NOWHERE. Nor can your ranger buddy be more than an arm's length away from you at any time. Get caught by a ranger instructor without your ranger buddy, and you receive a minor minus. Receive three of these minor minuses, and you have a major minus. Receive three major minuses, you pack your bags and head out, something no ranger student wants. No one goes in not genuinely wanting to pin on the coveted black-and-gold tab.

Adam was a first lieutenant and I was a sergeant (E-5) when we entered Ranger School. We only knew this because we told each other. (As I mentioned earlier, we don't wear rank in school.) In the "real world," I would salute Adam and call him "Sir" as he was a commissioned officer. In here, we were equals and had to have each other's back.

It's hard to explain how mentally engrossed you become in Ranger School. You basically forget about the outside world as you don't have phones, TV, or newspapers, and the RIs do not discuss the outside world around the students. I told my family and friends NOT to write me letters as I didn't want to be distracted from the goal. Although, letters typically weren't given out daily. But still, I wanted to stay completely focused. Adam and I were a great team and accomplished our missions almost with flying colors. It's often said that a ranger student will never pass their first graded patrol, but I still volunteered for the first assigned patrol, and I absolutely passed the first time! (You have to get three Patrol Leader "GOs" in order to graduate Ranger School.)

The point of this story is that Adam was my ranger buddy and had been from day one. About halfway through the mountain phase at RI changeover early one morning, a couple of instructors walked up to us and told Adam, Aka Ranger Such (pronounced Sook), that his wife was in labor with their first child and was having medical complications. Now, I know what you're thinking: this is a NO BRAINER situation, but you'd be wrong. You see, when put into certain living conditions and particular situations, a world that almost feels like a fantasy (and not the good kind of fantasy), can cause you to make decisions that are not rational. Adam actually hesitated for a few minutes before leaving. Not because he didn't love his wife and soon-to-be-born child with his entire heart and soul, but because his thinking and way of life were wholly reconditioned from what he had known. He had become laser-focused on the mission, and that mission was to graduate from this school and pin that tab as so few have done.

Anyway, I used to be ashamed to even admit this, but I'm not anymore. I was deeply depressed after Adam left because I felt like I had lost an appendage. It's like any great relationship, like the one I have as I write this with my wife, Angie. I absolutely can't completely function without my wife, which is why we're such a great team. You see, Ranger School taught me more than anything else that I could have possibly learned that being part of a cohesive team is *the* most essential thing in life.

I never saw Adam again, nor do I know what happened to him. I pray he came back, graduated Ranger School, pinned the tab, and lived a very successful life.

Swamp Phase
Conducted at Camp James E. Rudder at Eglin Air Force Base and hosted by the Sixth Ranger Training Battalion, this is the semi-amphibious and waterborne part of training. River crossings, small boat movements, and all manner of water-based actions are learned here. Naturally, the rigor and hunger inflicted on the students had been compounding too, so we were sore, hungry, tired, and fundamentally exhausted by the time we reached this point. I was more worn out than I ever had been in my life by the time I made

it to the swamp. The capstone event is a raid against the OPFOR on an island.

The OPFOR scenario intensifies, and we start focusing on "in-country" training: operating when you are deep into hostile territory. Raids, ambushes, pushing to engage, and urban assaults all play out here, as the squad is forced to work as a team to overcome the enemy. And the "enemy," in this case, are graduated Rangers, eager to test themselves against the armed forces' best up-and-comers.

By the time the swamp phase was over, my company was truly ate up! Ate up means we had a severe case of dumbass. We lost so many ranger students that our company was disbanded, and those of us who remained were doled out to the remaining companies. Many of you won't believe this, but I swear it's true. Swamp phase, at the time I went through, was seventeen days, with one day, in the end, being part of our one and only eight-hour break in the entire course. For fifteen days, our company was so messed up that we never reached the last priority of work, which is sleep. SLEEP! This is the reason we lost so many students. Now I'm not saying that I never slept. I'm sure while I was lying in a security position which was always, my head would slowly fall down, and my forehead would rest on the carrying handle/sights of my M16 rifle. Soon after, a ranger instructor would be kicking my ribs through to the next phase, screaming, "Wake up, Ranger!"

To which you'd raise your head and say with complete confidence, "I'm not sleeping, Ser'eant!"

Yes, I spelled that correctly. No one says s
phonetically correct; Rangers leave out the *G*. (ι
know.) Of course, you have this deep indentation froι
M16 sights on your forehead, which made you guilt,
charged. Now, the RI could give you a minor minus for
incident, and most of the time, they did. Hence, we lι
almost our entire company.

I would love to give you some great words of wisdom on
how I was such a superhero and made it through this phase.
But honestly, I genuinely believe this was just the grace of
God. And although I could be a better witness, make no
mistake, I talk to God daily. Always have, and I always
will. I suggest you do the same.

Desert Phase

I can see the finish line, and yet it seems so far away!
Designed and implemented relatively recently, by the time I
went through the desert phase, the thing had only been
running consistently since '83. Here, we learned basic
desert survival techniques, like how to get water, water
preservation, heat mitigation, and poisonous and venomous
animal awareness. Airborne assault is covered here too. As
a matter of fact, we jumped into Dugway, Utah, for desert
phase, and it was SNOWING! I mean, I hate cold weather
as it is but snow? I mean, come on, Lord, what possible
lesson could you be trying to teach me? I really did feel like
this was going to be the end of me. Not because I was
afraid to jump; I loved jumping. But it was extremely cold.
I was concerned that my hands wouldn't be able to operate
correctly should I need them. Well, I made the jump, landed

without breaking anything, made it out of my T-10 parachute gear and shoved it in the bag, and somehow made my way to the turn-in point.

The very first mission that we did, we were in a large *V* formation moving across a vast, open high plains' dessert. Just as I started thinking that this was a "piece of cake," the RI threw several smoke grenades and yelled, "GAS! GAS! GAS!"

This is meant to simulate a chemical attack, and you must don your protective mask within nine seconds. Once the mask is on, you resume your mission. There are other NBC (Nuclear, Biological, and Chemical) tasks that must be performed, but I'll spare you the details. Ultimately, over the next several clicks (kilometers), we would end up in full MOPP (Mission Oriented Protective Posture) gear, which is surprisingly warm, so I must admit I didn't hate it. It sucked to walk in, but it was warm.

Dress for the weather, people! Mountains and some climates or seasons have temperatures that can change rapidly. Even if you don't wear it, bring warm clothes. It would be best if you had blankets in your trunk along with the spare tire.

By the time all the phases are over, it's graduation time. Held at Victory Pond, the black-and-gold Ranger Tab is pinned to the left shoulder by a relative; conversely, maybe an RI or soldier from your unit does the honors. Whoever puts it there, it usually stays for your entire career, right

over your unit patch. For me, it was my dad. I graduated from Ranger School on December 12, 1989, and my mom, dad, aunt, and uncle attended. Once the ceremony was nearly over, my dad was asked to come out on the field, and he pinned on my tab. Of course, it was raining and cold, so one side of my face was purple. I mean, I love the cold, right? Geesh. I must admit that even to this day, this has been my greatest accomplishment. Rangers Lead the Way!

Looking back over the history of Ranger School now, it is no surprise that most of the fatalities have been hyperthermia. What raised my eyebrows was learning that one of the first deaths in '77 was during the swamp phase in Florida! Hypothermia is no joke, and people always want to assume it can only happen in extremely cold conditions, but all you need is water and a lower ambient temperature than your body. Soggy clothes keep your metabolism from keeping you warm enough, your core heat falls below what you can survive, and the body begins to shut down. It looks like after I left, a few more fatalities—again in the Florida swamps—led them to make some changes to how they run the swamp phase. Oh, but don't worry. It's mostly just environmental monitoring, so nobody else freezes to death. Ranger School is still one of the most challenging schools on the planet.

I mentioned the hunger before, but let me drill down a bit. When I went to Ranger School, you'd only eat an average of one MRE a day, which is even more challenging because they do not have a lot of calories in the first place. Just imagine only eating one meal in a day, and a crappy one at that. Usually, the only chance we'd get to eat was at RI turnover. RI turnover is when the ranger Instructors change out over their twenty-four-hour shift, typically at six in the morning. The person overseeing the platoon gets refreshed every twenty-four hours, but we sure as hell don't. So, when the RIs switched out, that was the only time we were allowed to eat.

Sometimes, you walk as much as ten to fifteen kilometers in a day, all on one scrappy little MRE you scarfed down at 6:00 a.m. On top of that, you're laden with gear—your rucksack plus your LBE—that can weigh anywhere between forty and eighty pounds. LBE stands for load-bearing equipment, which consists of two canteens, ammo pouches, first aid pouch, possibly hand grenades, and any other ammo, night-vision goggles, or weapons that you may be carrying. Hungry and tired, it's a long hard slog to get anywhere. You *can* carry as much water as you need, within reason, because they don't want people passing out, but you have to be careful. It's not like they follow you around with a cooler, and you can't just go dipping into the creeks or rivers either as you will get sick.

Sometimes, if you screwed up, delayed, or had any kinds of problems with your mission, they might come in and say, "Hey, you have to work through chow." That's another twelve hours without eating. At 6:00 p.m., they *may* let you at the MRE. The worst-case scenario is that you have to go all night *again*, making you wait a full forty-eight hours before you eat. That was the most prolonged period I had to endure; other ranger students might have different stories. The more you mess up, the more likely it is that you'll never achieve the priority of work that is chow. It's not cruel or abusive, because if you screw up in wartime, people die; missing a meal only drives the point home of how important it is to be organized and prepared. Screw up in an active war zone and missed sleep will be the least of your worries.

A little bit of experience with hunger is essential training, not just for self-mastery and discipline, because there are quite possibly situations in an active theater where you won't get to eat for days. Adrenaline and urgent need are a hell of a motivator, and real-time experience with all of these possibilities is important to make sure they don't get the better of you when they come up. Never having gone through one day without missing a meal is quite common, so knowing how to push past that is crucial to a military outfit. Not only missing a meal, but exerting yourself, raiding, ambushing, digging fox holes, and moving overland via LPCs (leather personal carrier = boot), all on an empty, and even painful, stomach burns so many calories it's insane.

Doing all that on a single MRE is bad enough. It was so long ago, but I want to say that over the nine weeks, I lost around forty pounds, and I didn't have it to lose in the first place! I came out of ranger school looking like a skeleton.

It's probably clear by now why the washout rate is so high. Remember, it is a leadership academy, right? They have to do what they can to simulate combat situations without actually dragging ranger students into a real war zone. Historically, commanders with no real wartime experience have been the root of some of the most significant defeats. Stress from hunger, sleep loss, or enemy actions all adds up. Compounding disaster on top of disaster, you need some familiarity with pushing past problems that are out of your control so you can get a grip on what you can. By the way, I may be telling you about what I learned in Ranger School; however, by now, you should see the correlations in your own life.

So when they put you in charge of completing a mission with somewhere between ten and fourteen men, you have to find a way to motivate them to get the show on the road, which is not an easy task when your humping sixty pounds fifteen clicks through rolling terrain on an empty stomach without having slept in days. Those squads we learn to command aren't getting graded, so they don't really give a crap. Tired, hungry, and sore, they'd often balk and sometimes not do what I needed them to do. It's a leadership course, so I had to get creative in leading them. Let me tell you, when you're dealing with a soldier in the army, more carrot less stick is an understatement. We're not actually allowed to hit anyone anymore, and that never gets the desired result, anyway. Since it is a simulated combat zone, it's not like they have a lot a leader can use by way of a metaphorical carrot, anyway.

Motivation can come in many forms, and it's when we are at our most exhausted, when it feels like we just want to lay down and die, that the tough get going. It is always better to lead by example. My hardheaded ability to push forward no matter what helped my men get moving far more than any yelling, threatening, or bribing that I could muster. Training a dog is faster and more effective if you treat the desired behavior, not punish the bad, and it is true in people too. We all crave accolades and praise; nobody wants to feel like a punk. One must lead with an open hand, not a closed fist, if you will.

I could not choose to not lead them because it's not just about earning a pass in ranger school. You can actually lose points toward the goal. There are things called major minuses, if you remember, that I mentioned briefly earlier in the chapter. It would be like if a teacher could give you a negative mark: *F* Minus. It is actively lowering your grade. While it was some time ago, I remember that you get booted if you get three Majors. In a combat scenario, failure to lead will get your men killed because that's precisely the outcome in the real world. Remember: an incompetent boss repels competent workers at best and kills the business at worst.

Getting pissed-off soldiers to do what they need to do is the essence of ranger school, in my opinion, and a good deal of the learning curve was massaging egos and identifying emotional states as much as it was survival and combat training. It's not herding cats but shepherding lions. As difficult and cantankerous as many of them were, I found overcoming the challenges and obstacles invigorating. Well, I was enthusiastic about everything I was learning, but as invigorated as I was, I was not full of vigor by the time I graduated!

Dugway, Utah, was our final phase: the desert phase. Now back then, you had what was called a "live fire" week, where you'd train with real tracer rounds flying overhead from M60 and .50 caliber machine guns. I don't know if they do this anymore, but I will tell you that it had a pucker factor of a solid ten! Now, it might have been twenty or thirty feet above us but taking the objective under those conditions takes a tenacity that's hard to find. Leading others through the same takes a charisma that's hard to teach or train.

As I said earlier, I graduated on December 12, 1989, making me a "Winter Ranger." One part of the swamp phase took place in the Florida panhandle (it was still freezing to me), but it was cold as hell for most of the course. In fact, the last phase, the desert phase, is where we jumped into about seven to eight inches of snow. I was miserable, to say the least. Remember, I grew up, was stationed, and rocked out in warmer climates. I was not used to cold like that. But they trained us the best they can on how to survive plunging temperatures, and those that couldn't cope washed out due to cold weather injuries. So, as far as the memories go, ass-biting cold included, it was another excellent learning experience. However, you couldn't pay me good money to do it again!

After ranger school graduation, I would stay and serve in the RIP detachment for a few years. The RIP liked my previous experience, and First Sergeant Jesse Laye, who was in charge of the detachment, all but made me stay. He said that he only wanted me to stay if I wanted to, but I pretty much didn't have any choice in the matter. I'm happy I stayed as it was a great assignment. I didn't know it at the time, but it would lead to one of my army career's most outstanding duty assignments. Now and then, someone spotted an aptitude in you that you might not have recognized. I find it always pays to stop and at least consider the idea; we have massive blind spots when we try to look at ourselves, and taking another's point of view at face value can be educational all on its own!

While serving at RIP and being a part of the Seventy-Fifth Ranger Regiment, I was deployed on a combat operation as part of a security team for a special operations unit out of Fort Bragg. While on that mission, doing quite frankly a boring job of laying in elephant grass performing security for AH-6 Little Birds (helicopters), I met a couple of operators and struck up a conversation. Long story short: when I got back to Benning, I received a secure call from Fort Bragg from a recruiter in The Unit asking me if I wanted to try out and interview for The Unit. Of course, I jumped at the chance.

Now I'm telling you all of this not because I'm trying to convince you that I'm some badass; I promise you I'm not a bragger. I even got the job despite the command sergeant major of the ranger regiment saying that, at the time, I wasn't going anywhere because they were critically short. My recruiter from Bragg told me not to worry. I had orders cut to be reassigned to "the army's highest priority tactical unit."

Made famous by Hollywood and variously glorified or vilified in the press, Delta Force is an elite strike force that many have heard of but don't really know much about. Founded in 1977 to specifically fight terrorism, Delta Force operates under the Joint Special Operations Command, meaning we get a little Air Force, a little army, a little Navy, and a little of whoever gets brought in for special missions. It was a great assignment, I worked with some of the most outstanding men and women that have ever served this great nation, and it was indeed a privilege. Life lesson learned? GO FOR IT! Is there something out there you think you can't have? That you can't accomplish? I promise you that you'll never know until you go ALL IN and *bite off more than you can chew!*

One last quick story! I did get a plaque from the men I served with in the Seventy-Fifth. Etched onto a small brass plate amongst my master wings, Combat Infantryman's badge, etc., are the words "Nobody Can Kick Your Ass." Now, this should obviously not be true. Well, maybe not obvious. This quote was all because of a single occasion at a bar in town one night. Several of my ranger buddies and I had been drinking for a while, and right before the last call, this huge guy started talking smack to me and trying to pick a fight. He was massive, looming over me like a gorilla. At some point, he shouted, "I'm gonna kick your ass!"

Keep in mind; this knucklehead was TWICE my size! I'm tiny compared to him.

I stepped forward, never breaking eye contact, and say, "Nobody can kick my ass."

I said it with a low tone and a crazy kind of serial killer voice. Who knows, maybe I did have a death wish, but I knew that I was sick and tired of bullies. Just because they thought they were bigger and tougher and could get away with picking on people, they did, and (as you've already read), this was a task I had handled before. Still, we were in totally different weight classes; while I was no welterweight, this dude was heavy, for sure.

I patiently waited for my head to be removed from my shoulders, but the blow never came. I had never risen to bait like this, at least not since the Ralph incident I outlined in chapter one. But it was clear he meant to attack.

He just stared at me with his face shaking in anger and backed up.

"You're fucking CRAZY!" Then he turned and walked away. I would not get my butt handed to me that night but learned once again just how important it is to stand up to your enemies and your fears; usually, that's all it takes.

Because of this episode, when The Unit threw me a going-away party for my next duty assignment in special operations, they had the words engraved on the plaque.

Without knowing the story, it makes me look like a hard-ass, To those in the know (that is YOU, too, now), it was just a crazy act of extreme courage or something that could have been a terrible regret. Either way: I'm proud of being a Ranger.

Mountain Ranger

After serving three years at Fort Bragg in special operations, I decided that I wanted to spend some time serving with my brother, Darryl. He was assigned to the Fifth RTB (Ranger Training Battalion) in Dahlonega, Georgia, in the north Georgia mountains. As long as you've served successfully in special operations, you can choose your next duty assignment provided there's a slot. There was, and that's where I went. I spent the next three years at Camp Frank D. Merrill before my branch selected me for recruiting.

Recruiter

When I was selected to be a recruiter, I must tell you that I was *not* very happy. As a matter of fact, I tried my hardest to fight DA (Department of the Army) on it but to no avail. And then, on top of that, after spending twelve weeks at recruiting school in Indiana during a summertime heatwave, they assigned me to the Tampa Recruiting Battalion in Winter Haven, Florida: land of the GED.

Now, I have nothing against a GED, but at the time I was recruiting, the army wasn't allowing anyone to join that didn't have a high school diploma. Winter Haven is in the middle of nowhere in Central Florida. When kids

64

graduating from high school left for college, it was Orlando to the east, the University of South Florida in Tampa to the west, college down south in Miami, or north to Tallahassee. Everyone else that wasn't qualified to join? Well, they just stayed right there in good ol' Winter Haven. This sealed my fate of working seven days a week, twelve-to-fourteen-hour days, talking to hundreds of men and women each month just to recruit—wait for it—a grand total of TWO qualified enlistees! Oh, dear God, how ridiculous it was trying to find qualified folks to join. But little did I know when I started down this road, it would end up being the one thing that would give me a taste of something I would want to sink my teeth into for the rest of my life!

Why Would I do Well at This

For one thing, I had done very well in the military, earned more badges, ribbons, and medals than would typically fit on my chest. OK, maybe a bit of a stretch, but I did have some weight pinned on. My crisp smile, friendly nature, and decorated uniform all gave me something to talk about. The medals and patches worked as talking points as well, giving me some interesting options to throw around, including the Ranger Tab over my unit patch, two different patches on my right shoulder: the 82d Airborne Division and the Seventy-Fifth Ranger Regiment, both for serving in combat with the units. Put all that together along with a blouse, spit-shined jump boots, and a black beret, and I could actually draw crowds to my recruiting tables that were set up at the local community colleges or one of the several high schools that I was assigned to. People would want a picture taken, and the vibe really came to remind me of my rockstar days. I had done it again; I had found myself the center of an appreciative audience!

It was my first real "selling" job, and I was selling the most challenging thing you can sling: intangibles. What's that, you ask? Intangibles are things people buy, but they can't see, like a warranty for a car, a life insurance policy, health insurance, or a recruiting contract. Basically, I was selling people a lifestyle in the army, something they couldn't see, so I had to help them "see" what they were buying into. I was selling people the next four years of their lives; I was selling folks their future.

It isn't easy.

During my first year, though I had been through recruiting school, I learned as time went on that the army really doesn't know how to sell that well; hell, they even knew that. (I just said sell, well and hell- OK, just making sure you're with me) At this point, the army started sending me out to do formal sales training and formal professional development for public speaking, self-empowerment, and sales training. I was sent to sales courses hosted by Tony Robbins, Dale Carnegie, Lee DuBois, and more. Having already commanded the attention of hundreds from behind a guitar and led squads hungry, tired, sore, and pissed across the brutal terrain to victory, this kind of motivation and salesmanship came easy to me.

Learning how to kindle a spark of interest into a fire of passion takes as much intuition and luck as it does determination and empathy.

You must be ready, willing, and able to overcome "no," to hear the word as an indecisive *maybe* instead of a final verdict. Because people really do fire off judgments based on knee-jerk reactions, make broad declarative statements regarding topics they know very little about, and generally dismiss things out of hand far more than they actively think about them.

I forget where I learned it, but you can use a dismissive comment on their end to pivot toward an agreement with just a few well-placed words. They need to give you a reason, and not just a hard "No," but when they shoot you down, you pick up the thread of their words and start a dialogue. They thought they were shutting you off, but instead, they started a conversation. Now it would be rude to walk away. First, answer their rebuff as if they had responded positively. If they say, "No, I'm going to college."

You'd say something like, "Great! We pay for college and teach you skills that'll help you thrive there!"

Or if they say, "I'm just not the physical sort."

Your response would be, "Super, we'll whip you into shape; you'll be a pile of muscle by the time you get out."

Taking any rebuke in stride and learning how to spin it around and make it into a positive takes a little bit of practice. Still, once you get the hang of it, well, it's the reason people learn just to repeat "No" a bunch of times, not make eye contact, and keep walking past sales booths! A shrewd salesperson really won't take no for an answer as long as you are in earshot, but the best of us never make you hate us. All too often, people really *don't* know what they want until they see it, and my job was to make sure people understood precisely how the US invests in its military personnel.

It is hard to sell something you don't believe in, and my military career was as hairy as any. But overall, I feel my time there was well spent. As you can see, there was always a part of me that was a hellion, a bit of a rabble-rouser and boundary pusher. Had I not gone back to the armed forces when I did, it is entirely possible I would have ridden that lifestyle to its alcohol-soaked peak. While not every professional musician succumbs to addiction, the genre and era of music I was playing in were such that I knew I that I had to get out. I got the regulation and skills I needed to thrive, and now it was a simple matter of getting others to see how they could profit from enlisting.

I was pretty good at it. I became such a successful recruiter that it got me thinking about what I would be doing with myself after. All those motivational speakers were right: it was time to chart a path to fortune and personal fulfillment! I'd had a few ideas as to how I'd do that, but there was a part of myself that was holding back. In the words of the old army jingle, I had become All That I Could Be through the army. Becoming a ranger and working in a special operations unit was basically the peak for me, and I had no interest in retiring from the army. I had always said that once it wasn't fun anymore, I was walking. At fifteen years, that's precisely what I did.

At the end of my last enlistment of recruiting duty, I left the army and found myself back in civilian life. I started readjusting to normal life by buying a small cleaning franchise in Atlanta and a home in Dahlonega, Georgia. If you recall, this is where I was stationed for the mountain phase of ranger school. I loved the town and thought it would be great living there.

However, I could not have been more wrong in my assessment. Here's the thing: I'm not trying to write a biography here. My goal is to tell you parts of my life in which I overcame some adversity and learned something that I can pass on. Maybe research as much as you can before buying into an area you are not intimately familiar with? Knowing the demographics and competition in the area a bit more would have been beneficial at least.

In any case, all I'm going to say is that because things weren't going as planned, it put me in a position to travel back and forth to NC doing some painting jobs for my dad. He was a project manager for a large commercial construction company in Raleigh, NC at the time. These odds and ends painting jobs would put me right where I was supposed to be for the next significant chapter of my

life. And I most certainly bit off more than I could chew!
Or so I thought . . .

CHAPTER 5: "MONEY"

Pink Floyd; 1973

Have the Courage to Do the Impossible

One of my odd jobs was painting a McDonald's—yes, the burger place. It was at that job site, standing in line for lunch, that I struck up a conversation with this really well-dressed man. A new suit and tie, nice shoes, a thousand-watt smile, and really white teeth that put mine to shame. He was struck right away by my articulation and general bearing, telling me right there in line at the fast-food joint that my talents were being wasted and I should really give him a call. I told him that I didn't work at McDonald's and pointed out my painting supplies; it was something I grew up doing, and I was most certainly between careers. Although I did tell him that I made good money slinging a brush, he insisted I was wasting my abilities painting walls and gave me his card. He told me to give him a call soon and drove off in a nicer car than anything that I'd ever sat in.

His name was Lenny Black, and he had *just about* sold me an intangible. He was a financial advisor and had encouraged me to call him to apply for a position with his brokerage firm as a financial advisor as well. This requires taking the Series 7 Federal Stockbroker Exam, which isn't easy I might add. But it is something that would be required to become a licensed broker. Now you might be surprised to learn this, but I didn't immediately drop everything and pick up the phone. I pocketed his card, and while the idea rolled around my head for months, I didn't jump at the opportunity.

As much as I love my dad, and as much as I hold him up as one of the primary reasons I'm where I am today, nobody is perfect, and he shot the idea down without a second thought. When I told him with who I was thinking of applying, he just shook his head.

He said, "They only hire Harvard graduates."

Well, it never occurred to me this might be false. My old man is blue-collar and a very hardworking man. Practical, maybe a little stubborn, but definitely not infallible. Dad continued to tell me how his construction company had built out an office for an advisor, and they were a Harvard graduate.

"Our family just doesn't do that kind of work," he followed up with.

That kind of broad generalization should have tipped me off, but it was dad! We are all human, after all. I guess I'm falling all over myself rationalizing for him because I really do love the guy and hesitated including this part at all, but it is a crucial lesson: as much as I respect his advice, as much as you want to think the best of your heroes and role models, it is vital to double-check, verify, or otherwise corroborate information from anecdotal sources. Because it would take Mr. Black reaching back out to me to get this ball rolling.

Two months after running into him at the McDonald's, he called me out of the blue and asked if I was going to apply for the position. I replied that I hadn't, probably wouldn't, and that they only took Harvard grads anyway.

After a pause, where I was sure he was muted and laughing his head off, he assured me that they accept anyone who could pass the interviews (three of them) and required exams. At which point I said something about probably just not being cut out for managing investment portfolios anyway. The shrewd man that he is, rather than double down or make a rebuttal, went in the opposite direction.

"OK, Mike, you're probably right; there's no way you could pass the exams. I guess I must have misread your personality type, which I rarely do."

That was it. He said I couldn't do something. If there's one thing that appealed to my time in the military, it was demonstrating that I could do anything I set my mind to. Hitting a wall and overcoming it- literally in the case of the obstacle courses but symbolic, too. My already-confident attitude had been sharpened into a sense that I truly felt like I could do anything.

It's true, folks. As much as we tell ourselves otherwise, like Doc Brown says in *Back to the Future*, "If you put your mind to it, you can accomplish anything."

So, I applied, and over the course of several weeks, I went through three different interviews. And, finally, I was offered a position. The fun started as the very first hurdle was to pass the Series 7 exam. This is a six-hour, 250-question test broken down into two parts with a mandatory thirty-minute break in the middle. (I'm sweating just thinking about it!)

I would dig into those Series 7 study guides like an animal, spending the next eight weeks knee-deep in the rules and regulations surrounding the buying, selling, and maintaining diversified investment portfolios. I learned about stocks, bonds, mutual funds, and all the other paper-dry strategies people employ to make their money work for them and to make even more money.

See, for all my dad's strengths, he, like so many of us, are stuck in thinking about money as an inert thing or having a poverty mindset. In a savings account, money is idle—stagnant. People lose sight of the root of the word currency: current. To some degree, liquid assets are meant to be on the move, like a river flowing or an electrical circuit. Unfortunately, using money to make money does usually require a fairly sizable amount to get started. Granted, one can work their way up from small investments to managed portfolios and more, but you have to be really disciplined.

In any case, eight weeks after Lenny's reverse psychology phone call and then getting hired, and THEN studying for another eight weeks, I took the Series 7 exam and passed. Also known as the General Securities Representative Exam

(GSRE), this test is required to become a Registered Representative. The Financial Industry Regulatory Authority, or FINRA, puts it on. If you are going to buy, sell, and manage security products in the US, you must go through them. Stocks, corporate and municipal securities, direct participation programs, investment products, real estate investment trusts, and variable contracts. It is all just mind-numbingly dull to most, but it is the heart of knowing the job as well as another battlefield, once you get into it.

In a dynamic environment, it pays to keep moving. Stand still for even a moment, and the quick will pass you by, the opportunistic will exploit you, and the evil sons of bitches will try to take you out. Financially speaking, very few concepts apply to war that doesn't carry over to the business world. That's why so many barons of industry read *The Art of War* and other books on military strategy. Competitors are the opposition, and overcoming the objective means taking their market share at a minimum. Buying them out or putting them out of business is about as close to "killed in action" as a civilian is likely to get.

If you get a wild hair and decide to try your hand at becoming a broker, just know that while anyone can take it, you do have to be sponsored by a member firm (brokerage firm) or a self-regulatory organization.

"You're So Lucky!"

My first year as a stockbroker went fast. If you don't know what they do, it's basically managing a collection of financial investments and making recommendations for your client. You watch markets all day, stay nimble, and buy or sell into or out of the portfolio in response to what the indexes are doing. Based on the agreements you make with your client, your investments will be a careful balance between fluid and open to speculation and locked up in bonds and more or less stable. Brokers earn a commission, markup, or fee for their services. The better you manage the account, the more money it makes and the more profit we make.

I was able to drum up new investors because I was not afraid to literally knock on doors. Knowing you miss 100 percent of the shots not taken, I took to the streets and beat the pavement, running around like a crazy person and finding that, sure, ninety-nine people might shoot you down, but 1 percent of them say "maybe." Do that all week, all month, all year, and hash those dozens of *maybes* into a routine of casual but urgency-building phone calls, and you have yourself a burgeoning client list. This is sales 101 and a rule for life all at the same time: Ask. State your intent. Be direct and remain pleasantly persistent. Build urgency by explaining timeliness and time-sensitive opportunities.

At the annual awards ceremony after my first year there, I won The Prospecting Award, Rookie of the Year Award, and The Regional Leaders Award, along with several more. Being a low man on the totem pole, a "rookie broker," I was seated in the back of the room, but I burned that carpet up going to and from the podium all night accepting awards. I kept walking past this one guy and eventually caught his eye a few times. Well, I don't know if he was feeling jealous or just being glib, but when I passed him, at some point near the end, he leaned over and said, "You're so lucky!" I went up, got my award, and sat back down at my table. My mentor, an awesome man, Bowie Martin, leaned over and smirked.

"Isn't it crazy how we create our own luck?"

I've never forgotten those words to this day and have created my own luck now for decades!

Luck is funny like that. Because while there is certainly something to be said for good fortune, you can't rely on it. And as counterintuitive as it sounds, you really *can* make your own luck. I'm not talking about anything supernatural like karma or even prayer (well, prayer for sure is a must) but just a set of best practices that can be employed to get you living your best life.

Making Your Own Luck

First, you have to place yourself in a position for good things to happen to you. No one is going to knock on your door and offer you a job; you must be out there hustling. (For the record, I love the word hustle!) Be aware of the quality of the activity you are trying to be a part of and seek its higher end. You've heard the expression "shoot for the moon, so even if you miss, you land among the stars." It applies to us all universally. Chase your dream job, pursue that seemingly impossible goal, and aim for the highest mark you can possibly achieve. Even if you land on your face, it will be a few steps closer than you were.

Next, you cannot give up. You hear it again and again, but it's something few people have the stomach for. Failing, getting back up, and trying again can be grueling. Sometimes it can feel like no progress is being made, but as long as you're trying new approaches and changing your technique, trust me, you're growing! Don't keep trying the same thing again and again, hoping for a different result. You know, the popular definition of insanity? Sometimes it's a matter of practice, and all you can do is keep trying. But more and more in this life, the victory goes not to the smartest, fastest, and most able, but the ones who picked themselves up and kept going again and again, the ones who learn from their mistakes. One of my favorite scenes is from the sixth *Rocky* movie, *Rocky Balboa*, and I watch the video often. Here's the script:

> *"The world ain't all sunshine and rainbows. It is a very mean and nasty place, and it will beat you to your knees and keep you there permanently if you let it. You, me, or nobody is gonna hit as hard as life. But it ain't how hard you hit; it's about how hard you can get hit and keep moving forward. How much you can take and keep moving forward. That's how winning is done. Now, if you know what you're worth, then go out and get what you're worth. But you gotta be willing to take the hits, and not pointing fingers*

saying you ain't where you are because of him, or her, or anybody! Cowards do that, and that ain't you. You're better than that!"
                                        – Rocky Balboa

Man, I wish I could have written that! I mean, it's true!

Look, you have to work for it! There's absolutely no substitute for hard work. Elbow grease, spit, and vinegar; vim and vigor. More intangibles: proof perhaps that the best things in life are free is that your effort to make those best things happen is what *makes* them happen. Silver Spoons, trust funds, and inherited wealth notwithstanding, your hard work is what gives material possessions their worth. Having worked with some extremely wealthy people, I can tell you that those who were born into big money are just as prone to depression, boredom, and feeling unfulfilled as any desperate wretch. That "money doesn't buy happiness" line always makes me want to scoff, but the truth is that money is no guarantee of happiness.

Lastly, for the love of God, just be nice to everyone. Or at least don't be an asshat. We all learned this one way or another in ranger school once rank was hidden; best to treat everyone as equals just to be safe. Even if the warmth of human companionship doesn't move you, there are selfish reasons to throw a little kindness around too. You quite simply never know who is going to do what in this life. That rude piece of crap that cuts you off or flashes you an attitude could be your future boss or someone that's just having a bad day. Someone might be on a razor's edge, and your simple interaction is all it takes to push them one way or another. We've all been there: at wit's end, frayed and taut, you are straining just to put one foot in front of the other, and some idiot blunders into your pet peeve, and you blow up.

Don't do that.

Especially don't do that to loved ones.

Taking frustrations out on those around you is bad form in any case but doubly so when it's friends or family. A little self-awareness goes a long way, and if you can't be trusted to aim your venting emotions away from the ones who care about you the most, then you're going to have a hard life. If you read the earlier chapters, you'll recall I said you shouldn't jam your emotions down? Well, sometimes it pays to do just that. Because in the same breath, I said, "or they'll run away with you." And getting salty with loved ones is that: feelings carrying you away. If you rile and rage at the closest targets instead of the causative ones, the integrity of your relationships will be collateral damage in the end.

Emotional intelligence isn't just valuable for interpersonal communication, but overall life. Maintaining a certain dispassion when working with portfolios is necessary, as it is with any complex system. You can't get spooked, fall in love, or let yourself hate a company, client, or security option. If you do, you must be able to operate and remove yourself from the intense emotions, mindful, of course, as to *why* it is playing on your feelings the way it is while being able to move through it.

Knowing "when to hold 'em, when to fold 'em, when to walk away, and when to run" would bring me to one of the nation's largest brokerage firms. I'll keep their name out of the book for no other reason than me possibly pissing them off. I mean, I really shouldn't because I worked there for several years with distinction and left on good terms. Regardless, it's one of the biggies whose name you hear before public television shows or uttered with gravity from the TV when the markets are turbulent. I was good at my job, but for as long as I worked for the big boys, there was one threshold I would never break in the short time I was there: the 10K in a Month club.

Try as I might, I couldn't hit the near-mythic ten thousand dollars of income in a month, a mark of a high-ranking broker's ability and no small amount of status around the company. While it was rare for a first, or even a second-year broker to meet that level of income, I was sure I could do it. I would wind up hitting this target, but it would be working under my own independent administration. There was no award when I hit this mark beyond the sense of having accomplished alone what I couldn't do working for someone else. My excuse is because the commission structure was set up to take care of the house and not the broker as much. However, I am getting ahead of myself.

During the time I was with the firm, I was "knocking on doors" a LOT and doing a lot of business-to-business prospecting. My life in the military had prepared me for it, though, so when many of my fellows were quailing under the burden of being up before the sun and working way past dusk, I was perfectly fine because no one was shooting at me and my stomach was full. I would beat the streets, drumming up new investors as we begin the daily care and maintenance of diversified investment portfolios. Mutual funds, bonds, fixed and variable annuities, and of course, stocks. I knew people would be needy with their nest egg and equity on the line, but I was not prepared for just how fickle folks can be. Never happy and seldom satisfied. While most of my clients were OK, a few contacted me all the time; this got even more intense at the end of the ˙90s.

If you recall, 1999 was a crazy time for the stock market. Y2K had spooked some of the population, and the market being as prone to rumor and superstition as your typical middle school kid, it was jumpy too. Now, we had a pretty strong policy at the time of buy and hold, where you buy into stocks from entities that are large enough to bounce back from anything, and when the going gets tough, you hold, and once everything normalizes again, everything is fine.

Well, I didn't agree with this.

I always disagreed with that policy; I called it Buy and Hope because you are essentially betting on everything staying as it was or "hoping" the devaluation of your stock portfolio or other investments would just bounce back. Well, I have news for you: your stocks don't know that you own them, and they're not coming back for you just because you want them to. If there's one thing they drill into your head at all stages of military training, it's that the battlefield is a living thing, and the best-laid plans can go straight to hell as soon as your boots hit the dirt. Locking yourself into a set course of action just because that's how you planned it and not changing it even though it's become clear it is no longer a good idea is ridiculous in my opinion. There's not a single piece of military strategy that has ever survived an encounter with the enemy. Eisenhower may have been talking about war, but it's true to any plan you care to make.

In March of 2000, after basically a ten-year bull market run in the '90s, what goes up must eventually come down, and the stock market started to correct.

I had this one retired couple who came in to see me one afternoon concerned about their retirement portfolio. Granted, they were naturally in conservative investments. Being retired, they wanted as steady and as safe a revenue stream as possible, but even conservative investments were taking a beating. I did the compliant thing and recommended that they just try to relax as their money was diversified and the portfolio taking on some water, so to speak, was normal. They weren't buying that strategy and basically said that they would seek another advisor if I couldn't help keep them from losing money.

Going against the compliance policy of the brokerage firm I worked for, which was to buy and hold, I recommended moving all their long (stock) investments into a money market, which was paying 7 percent at that time, and into some short-term managed bond funds that were in the same family of funds they were already invested in. Bonds work inversely of stocks; usually, bonds go up in value when stocks are declining. Not much, but this strategy provides a "floor" for the portfolio and stops the bleeding. Since the money was sheltered INSIDE of a retirement account, then selling off the stocks had zero tax consequences, nor was there a commission or a cost as I kept them in the same family of funds. (I hope this is making sense.) Within two weeks, the losses that their portfolio had taken had already been made up, and they started telling all of their friends and family. Now, there was a little more technicality to managing the portfolio, but hopefully, you understand. And you see, anytime you take money out of mutual funds that are invested in stocks, the brokerage firm stops making Trails (money). Just imagine hundreds of millions of dollars in funds making money, and then one of your brokers starts moving the money out. I can see why the firm wasn't keen on me doing this. Hence, I was threatened on more than one occasion to be terminated if I kept doing it. Well, I did just that. I moved most of my retirement clients into safer investments, and I'm glad I did because this was dubbed the Dot-Com Crash and lasted until 2002. When it was all said and done, the S&P had fallen 45 percent, and to make matters worse, we somehow had a brief recession smack dab in the middle!

It turns out I didn't get fired, but I most certainly pissed a lot of people off that I worked for. What can I say? They still liked me for some odd reason.

As thankful as I was for the opportunity and friendships I made, I resigned and started my own independent brokerage firm. The hardest part about making the decision to leave was leaving my book of business; that belongs to the brokerage firm when you're an employee. It took me three years to build, and I was walking out on it. Now, there was a legal way without risk of being sued where I could send out a letter to my clients and simply thank them and let them know that I was leaving. You can't tell them where you're going, nor can you solicit their business. And the truth is most of my client base stayed right there with the firm, and I completely understand that. But a few dozen searched for me and moved their accounts to my surprise. I mean, I'm now basically a one-man show and a startup, so they were taking a considerable risk. (I did hang my hat with an independent brokerage house, meaning the clients are now mine and not theirs.)

This would wind up being an excellent move for me personally because I felt unfulfilled, even though I was successful there. It was a feeling of "wrongness," though everything was going perfectly. At the time, I chalked it up to chaffing a bit because I'm so damned hardheaded sometimes under corporate leadership. Still, I not only survived, but thrived under some of the heaviest rules and overbearing compliance, in my opinion. You see, the lesson here is that many times in your life, you are going to work in environments that you may not agree with. My firm was 100 percent within their rights to run the company as they saw fit, and they had an impeccable record, or at least, they did at the time. So, although I had a fundamental disagreement with how they did things, it wasn't my name on the door. And yet, I still found a way to excel, and you must too! Learn everything that you can in every situation. Take notes, and at some point, the time will come to jump!

It was 2003, and I was once again a free agent.

CHAPTER 6: "YOU CAN GO YOUR OWN WAY"

Fleetwood Mac, Rumors; 1978

Leaving the Safety of the Known; Risking the Unknown

Feeling good about my prospects, I started my own practice, doing business as Michael Paulk – Retirement Planning. I was independent for several years, thriving now that I could call my own shots. Armed with a couple of years of experience and the slow trickle of clients I was finding (and found me from my last job), I struck out into the wild, unpredictable world of solo financial planning. My only other work experience in the private sector had been minor, independent contractor stuff, so I thought I might be ready, but it was a helluva transition. If selling yourself as an investment professional when working under the name of a major corporation is hard, doing so as a free agent can feel near impossible.

With the big company, it was easy to point at the top floors of the office building we inhabited, scheduled meetings in the glass and stainless-steel conference rooms, and otherwise use the clout of the multi-billion dollar company as proof. Then, all of a sudden, it was just me. Looking confident, being capable, and projecting charm is what got me from no to maybe, but my track record and knowledge of the marketplace allowed people to trust me with their

87

life's savings. So, with not a little bit of pushing past fear, I left another world-class organization of shit-kickers to pursue a loftier goal. Instead of the army, it was a world-class investment house, but instead of leaving for a somewhat abstract something else, I knew exactly what I was doing.

By hook or crook (it's an expression, I was never a crook!) and a lot of luck, the kind of luck you create as from chapter 4, I found success working as an independent advisor. It was here on my own, finally, that I breached the goal of well beyond 10K in profits a month, and I did this my very first month in business! This was an actual benchmark, and my previous firm gave out an award just for reaching it. Obviously, the longer you stay with a large firm, the more money you'll make, but the commission structure is a LOT smaller than being independent. I mean, so much of what was making me an excellent investment advisor was skilled learning through doing, so it was no surprise that I took off rather quickly. OK, that's not true; I was completely shocked at how fast I tasted success as an independent advisor.

Practical learning was always my strong suit over book learning, anyway. The army was nothing if not one long hands-on lesson. Even before that, learning guitar and making questionable decisions in the woods behind our house growing up, it was the physical lessons that sunk in the deepest. Still, I know how to plant my butt in a chair and get cracking when it's study time. An investment portfolio was just a unit of soldiers all over again: a squad of pushy, opinionated individuals, each with a mind of their own but capable of being called into order. Military metaphors have been largely avoided thus far, but I was hacking and slashing new paths toward financial stability, eliminating the occasional bad investment, and accomplishing profitable objectives. As I was applying myself to the world of financial planning with the same white-knuckled intensity I do everything else, my rapid growth and happy clients brought me to the attention of Fisher Investments in late 2006.

Now, a gentleman isn't supposed to talk about money, least of all the hard numbers. But I can't really get into the motivating factors here without brushing up against it a little bit. They were going to pay me 150K a year PLUS the commissions I'd get from clients. Usually, a broker works for commission *only*, so having a guaranteed take home *before* any commission was almost unheard of in this field. The only way they would hire someone at that rate was if they had earned a minimum of $150,000 in the previous year—which I had.

Again, this isn't to flash my bankroll but give you an idea of how much this job meant to me and how much was on the line. I mean, truthfully, if you know who Ken Fisher is in the world of investing, you'd understand. This man's a legend, and at that time, he'd already been writing a monthly article for Forbes magazine for over twenty years! He built his investment firm from the ground up to $20 billion in assets under management (AUM) in twenty years. He doubled that to over $40 billion in the next five years.

Today, as I write this in 2021, Fisher has over $188 BILLION in AUM! That's just plain nuts; that's all I can think to say. Ken is on the Forbes 400 Richest Men in America list with a net worth of over $4.3 billion dollars. Now you can't make a living on that, but it's a nice place to start. Am I right? Are you tracking my sarcasm? Alrighty then; moving along.

Living in Raleigh, North Carolina, at the time I was hired, my territory was going to be Eastern NC. However, when I showed up for training in Woodside, CA, they told me I'd be covering Tennessee. Tennessee? I was almost knocked off my feet, but if I wanted the job, then accepting the territory was the only way I was going to be a regional vice president for Fisher Investments. The thought of living on a plane wasn't as appealing to me after spending fifteen years in the army and exiting an aircraft in flight hundreds of times. But the benefits were considerable, not to mention the valuable experience I would gain, and of course, the company covers all travel expenses.

So, I went for it.

I spent two weeks in the company headquarters in Woodside, CA, going through extensive training and learning Fisher's sales process. It was awe-inspiring. Not simply the fact that they had flown me out here to learn, which was badass enough, but the campus they had us at was impressive. It was all comfy chairs and large projections, clean, well-lit spaces, and articulate but approachable instructors. I wouldn't know it, but in the not-too-distant future (chapter 8, actually), I would be pulling from this and other first-rate classrooms when it came time to do a little teaching of my own; but I got ahead of myself again!

Upon arriving back in NC, Fisher sent out some tech folks to set my home office up with a secure line for working on the PC with sensitive customer information. Usually, I started my weekly routine of flying to TN on Monday mornings and flying back to Raleigh on Thursdays or Fridays, depending on the number of appointments I had. I would usually take off at 8:00 a.m. and land in Nashville at 8:00 a.m. local time, gaining an hour flying out. I would grab my rental car and head straight to my first appointment. I would usually work my way down to Chattanooga for a day or so and then up towards Knoxville, where I'd fly out of back to NC. I passed by the Jack Daniels distillery a few times. That's all I'm saying about that; I'm more of a Scotch man, myself.

The minimum amount required to open a brokerage account at Fisher was 500K. Some of our larger clients were getting into the multi-millions. The *average* was $1.2 million, in my experience. So, to say there was a pretty good deal of equity flying around might be an understatement. If the stresses and pressures of keeping a squad of soldiers battle-ready and mobile were intense, it was a whole different kind of burden in this type of job. I remember my boss, who worked in the Woodside, CA, office telling me when I was first hired that this gig was a bit more for the "salty-dawg" type of salesperson. I think I knew what he was talking about, but I really just thought he needed to work on his analogies. Ha! He was a great guy, and I loved working for him at the end of the day. With great effort should come great reward, and I was seeing the kind of financial success I had dreamed about in my days of wanting to be a rockstar but never thought I'd get to.

My time with Fisher was rewarding, and some of the greatest moments of my finance career were with Fisher Investments. However, the same dissatisfaction for some unknown reason had gripped my heart, and by the end of 2007, I knew that it wasn't just working under a corporate flag that had worn me down too fast but the job itself. Yes, the constant flying and travel demanded of my Tennessee locale was part of it, but overall, I found the financial planning itself to be, quite honestly, unfulfilling. After all, it was a learning experience, and I made a mental checklist of what I had always enjoyed about brokering and what I was still looking for.

Working with people, yes. Dynamic, changing environment? Check. Making enough money to play and save; definitely. No more clients, though, or at least the sort of customers who don't call you all the time with endless crises both real and imagined. I was sick and tired of the road too, so whatever I did I knew I wanted it to have roots. The travel had been made even more burdensome by the addition in this part of the story with the love of my life, my best friend, most solid business partner, and beautiful wife since 2007, Angie.

While that is a story and a valuable lesson in itself (see chapter 7 below!), as far as it concerns what happened next, you only need to know I was no longer feeling like an army of one but more a piece of a whole. And my other half was in North Carolina!

So while I woke up one day and decided the investment world wasn't bringing me any satisfaction, it was a "straw that broke the camel's back" situation. Though instead of a small weight added to a great burden breaking a pack animal's stamina, it was a warm smile, kind eyes, and music-to-my-ears laughter that enticed me away from my life as a road-warrior salesman. Sounds straightforward, but I had been struggling with dissatisfaction for so long. Once I finally understood why, it was like a weight had fallen off my chest. That may sound a little harsh, but the world of managing people's money is never-ending, the miles were wearing on me; and then I found love.

I mentioned this above, but clients are fickle, never happy, and always demanding. OK, some are happy, and I did meet many great folks, and some are still friends to this day. But you're basically on call all the time for your clients. I'd get a ring if their portfolio was underperforming, of course, but then folks would get jittery when things were seemingly too good, also worried about crashes and bubbles. Even the packages I built specifically to be stable and hands-off would need a workover if requested. It got to be too much; a client watched a late-night infomercial on Gold or decided they wanted to go back to school. The more millions involved, the more frantic and end-of-the-world every call would be and the more entitled to special treatment they'd feel.

As I said, Fisher was excellent, and never did I have a "Take this job and shove it!" moment. One morning, it was more of a reflective moment, looking out over my breakfast at the day ahead, then seeing them stretch into the future. A sensation I know all too well took hold: it was time to look for greener pastures. The way ahead had to change; staying the course would either turn me into someone I didn't want to be or break me. I didn't reach any kind of breaking point as I had with the other or *Jerry Maguire* my way out of the office one day. Oh! That reminds me . . .

Speaking of *Jerry Maguire*, when I left my first firm to go independent, my very first client, and he's still a friend to this day, was a guy named Steve Crawford. Having gotten my farewell email, he called me up one evening out of the blue.

"Anyone that's got the balls to walk out of a major firm and venture out on their own has what I'm looking for; I'm all in! But first, you have to say the words."

I was confused by this.

"What words?"

"You know. If you're going to be like *Jerry Maguire*, then you have to say, '*SHOW ME THE MONEY!*'"

"You're joking, right?"

"Nope."

So sure enough, I had to yell into the phone, *"SHOW ME THE MONEY!"*

And he did just as he said he would! Steve is one of those guys that made the job great. He respected my experience and education and valued my opinions and tenacity. He was my client for many years until I bowed out of the industry. Again, we stay in touch to this day; sometimes the salesman really does like you and wants to be your friend.

Okay, back to our story already in progress: Leaving Fisher was an emotional decision, one I would unquestionably have ignored had I not learned how to pay attention to when my heart and mind were out of alignment. Again, though, not acting on impulse, but taking heed when the balance of my brain and body are trying to tell me something. If you're young or don't have quite as many obligations as I did then, I say go for it. Whatever "it" is. I would never have gone on to try my hand at rock and roll at this point; I did that when I had nothing to lose.

Walking away from a sure thing toward a great unknown can be difficult. No doubt, we had reservations, but once all was said and done, both my wife and I are practical idealists. We're both driven by dreams, and it sounds like dewy-eyed, unrealistic fantasies, but once you get into the habit, breaking an objective down into manageable chunks becomes second nature. Too often, I see people eye the destination and falter because they think it's too far. When it looks like the going is getting tough and you just wanna up and quit, look down to a smaller increment. Don't quail over the miles yet to go; celebrate the steps you've made. Because if nothing good comes easy, then the best things in life are worth working for.

If I hadn't taken a leap of faith leaving the main street USA firm when I went independent, I was about to fling myself out into space without a safety net. I would only find the strength through the love and support of my wife, but it would take everything I have learned to make my next career pivot. Everything I learned and the encouragement and support of my wife came together to give me the strength to leave yet another lucrative job, to change careers altogether. So, now I guess I'll tell you how Angie and I met.

In a romantic comedy, or other fictional stories, when boy meets girl, it's called a meet-cute, and a good story always has one. Where the protagonist and their crush run into each other in a humorous or affecting way, in another crazy example of my life imitating art, I was about to meet the future Mrs. Paulk while starting my transition out of Fisher.

CHAPTER 7: "HERE COMES MY GIRL"

Tom Petty and the Heartbreakers; 1979

It's Never Too Late for Love

I was traveling a *lot* for my job working with Fisher Investments in 2007. My territory was the state of Tennessee, and I lived in Raleigh, North Carolina. I would fly out Monday morning, usually around 8:00 a.m., and land in Nashville, Tennessee, around 8:00 a.m. local time. You lose an hour traveling west, so it was a net-zero loss. I conducted appointments all day in Nashville, Chattanooga, and more, ending up in Knoxville by Thursday or Friday. Then I'd catch a flight back to Raleigh for a day or two of rest, only to do it all over again.

I worked through most of the weekend, following up on appointments from the previous week and confirming appointments that were set for the next week, so maybe "rest" is too strong a word. However, it was worth it as the job paid extremely well, even if the hours and lifestyle were hell. As you can well imagine, I didn't really have much of a love life after all that.

What I did have was a profile set up on the Yahoo Personals dating site, so I could set up a dinner date here and there when I had time, which was admittedly rare. Like I indicated above, I wasn't looking for a wife. I had concluded that I would more than likely just be a bachelor the rest of my life; this is more evidence that remaining flexible in your thinking is a good idea!

I had also said that I was too old to have children at my age, forty-three at the time, so that would never happen. I didn't want to be in a relationship with a woman who had young children, I was at a stage of my life where freedom was important, and I most definitely was *not* going to get married again.

Yes, again. I had already been through a failed marriage when I was younger, and I didn't want to deal with that again. I would go into the details of that marriage, but honestly, the fallout of the divorce had long-lasting effects on some people, and to bring it up is just too personal at this time.

So, if you are observant, you'll realize I've said "never" three times now but also encouraged you never to say never!

Well, I was a Harley Davidson guy and rode every weekend and any other chance that I could. I've ridden motorcycles my entire life because it's the greatest feeling of freedom that I've ever experienced. I met a girl at Ray Price Harley Davidson one day (not a romantic interest), and she said to me that it was tough to find groups to ride with because she was black. I found it disturbing and sad, to say the least, and assured her that she could ride with my friends and me anytime she wanted. I gave her my number and told her to contact me any Friday, and I'd let her know where we'd be meeting up on Saturday to ride.

Several weeks later, I was in my apartment on a Friday evening after just getting in from Tennessee, and my cell rang; it was her. We proceeded to have a lengthy conversation and started talking about our bikes. The day we met, I was in my Jeep and didn't have my Harley with me. She asked if I had any pictures of my Softail Custom online; I said I did, but it was on my Yahoo Personals profile, and I currently had it hidden because I just didn't have time to date. Remember, this was before the age of smartphones, so I couldn't just pull out pics. She told me that she, too, had a profile and all I had to do was unhide mine for a little bit, and she could see the pictures of my Harley.

I signed onto the PC and clicked Show to make my profile visible, and we sat there talking about bikes for a while. Across town, there was something happening that would change my life forever.

This woman named Angie was with a friend of hers talking about online dating. Now Angie didn't have a profile on Yahoo, but her friend Tatum did. Tatum wanted to show Angie this guy that she was interested in (not me, someone else), but when Tatum signed into Yahoo Personals, *my* profile pic popped up first! Remember, I had just unhid my account minutes earlier! Angie asked who I was, and Tatum said just some guy that was obviously looking for someone.

She was evidently intrigued with my profile and decided to join Yahoo Profiles which I believed cost $29 at the time.

I mean, this woman paid money just to send me an email!

Meanwhile, back across town in my apartment, I'm about to hang up the phone with my friend and hide my profile again. Literally, a minute before I was about to hit the Hide button, I received an email alert. I only had my profile visible for maybe an hour or less! It was Angie. She saw my profile, created an account, and contacted me, all within approximately the one hour that my profile was visible! I remember her saying that she had uploaded a picture of herself, but Yahoo took at least twenty-four hours to approve pictures to ensure folks don't go against their set policies. She only said this because I had put on my profile that I expected one from anyone who contacted me since I had posted a pic.

I don't think I need to tell you that people will post a picture of themselves that's over a decade old, and they look *nothing* like it anymore. Oddly, for some reason, I just had a "feeling" that I would like this woman. I responded and told her no worries, and I thanked her for contacting me. We chatted back and forth that night via email to learn a little more about each other and did the same thing the next day. Ultimately, I told her that I wasn't looking for a pen pal and asked her to meet me for dinner or a drink. She explained how busy her life was and that it might take a little time.

You see, she had three young children, which was one of my "nevers." I would *never* date a woman with young children. But here I was, making an exception, so obviously, she was very special. Shocking no one, I'm attracted to active, busy people, and this gal was *busy*.

We set a date to meet two weeks later at the Carolina Ale House in Cary, NC, which was kind of halfway in between our two homes.

I later found out that she almost didn't show up!

She was a teacher in the Wake County Public School system and taught children with autism. This in itself made her a superhero in my eyes! Angie told her teacher assistants that she was probably going to back out of our date, but they really encouraged her to go, and thank God she did.

I remember leaning up against a pole in front of the Carolina Ale House the night of our date, March 21, 2007. There was this long sidewalk leading up to the entrance where I was standing, and I swear to you that the second I saw her coming up the way, I said to myself, *I'm going to marry that woman.*

We met, went inside, and grabbed a table. It was the best date I had ever been on in my entire life! She was the most beautiful woman I had ever laid eyes on. We had so much in common that it didn't even make sense. It turned out that our paths had crossed so many times in our previous lives as we had lived in the same neighborhoods, went to the same bars, and followed the same bands. Her ex-boyfriend had even lived in a house *two* doors down from my younger brother and his family! That was just plain nuts!

At the end of the date, I asked her if I could take her to her car because it was cold out and she had parked a little far away. To this day, she says it was a ploy of mine just to get her in my Jeep—and it's completely true because I just didn't want the date to end! We then sat in my Jeep for a while and talked more. As I said, I didn't want the evening to end, but it was a weeknight, and she needed to work early the following day, as did I. It was also very rare that I was in town for the date because I was usually out of town for my job during the week. The truth is I made sure that I would be in town that week, as I was looking forward to meeting her. Nothing to me, for some reason (which is clear to me now), was more important than this date.

We were inseparable from that point on.

Again, we met for our first date on March 21, 2007, and were married exactly four months later to the day, on July 21, 2007, in Cocoa Beach, Florida. Now, you may not believe this, but I actually planned the entire wedding! I truly can't remember why, but I know it had something to do with Angie's schedule at the time. Honestly, it wasn't that big of a deal as I just contacted a company to set up everything on the beach for us at the Doubletree Hotel on Cocoa Beach. And my company at the time not only covered the cost of our hotel room, but they also covered the cost of our honeymoon. Full disclosure, we didn't really plan on a honeymoon in the beginning, but my company said if I'd conduct just one appointment in Virginia Beach, VA, they'd pay for our accommodations for that week. Boom! Instant honeymoon! That was fourteen years ago (as of the time of writing this book). I still worship every moment with her and tell her she's beautiful every single day and will until the day I die. If you don't believe in love at first sight, all I can say is it happened to me, and I'm beyond thankful.

Now you might be saying, what's this got to do with "Biting off more than you can chew?" Well, everything! You see, we really should never say never. I said "I would never" three times in reference to what I wanted in a relationship, and it was all wrong!

1. I would NEVER marry a woman with small children. When we met, Angie had three young children that I have had the privilege of helping to raise and, more importantly, receive their love. Not to mention we now have three grandchildren!

2. I said I would *NEVER* have a child of my own. Soon after our relationship started, we had the proverbial "oops." You know, the big surprise one month when she was "late." At first, it kind of bothered us because it's not what either of us thought we wanted. So when it turned out that she wasn't pregnant, I found myself a little sad, even disappointed. I wasn't sure if Angie felt the same way, but one evening soon after, we were talking, and she, too, in

fact, was a little unsure. Over the next couple of years, we suffered two miscarriages, a pain that's impossible to convey. I always knew what a miscarriage was, but I never completely comprehended the fact that it's losing your child, your baby. Just writing this brings tears to my eyes. My wife and I lost two babies that I look forward to meeting one day in Heaven. We kept the faith, and sure enough, the third time was the charm.

On March 9, 2010, at 5:14 p.m., our sweet baby girl, Mychael Eden Paulk (pronounced just like my name, Michael), was born. It was the absolute most incredible miracle I've ever witnessed in my entire life! Remember: I said I would "never" have a child of my own, and honestly, in hindsight, I can't imagine my life without my sweet baby girl.

3. I said I would never get married again. Well, by now, if you've been paying attention, you obviously know how that worked out. I married the absolute love of my life! The woman I'm convinced that God sent to save me from myself, to help give my life purpose and direction, a reason to live life to the fullest! I love, adore, and quite frankly, worship the ground my wife walks on.

Do you see? I absolutely bit off more than I *thought* I could chew! It's incomprehensible to me what I would have lost in my life had I not taken the chance or if I'd been too afraid to take risks. Please, don't be scared of the unknown, because in my opinion, humble but accurate, that's where life begins!

CHAPTER 8: "SHARP DRESSED MAN"

ZZ Top; 1983

Stepping Onto Stages Helping Others

Like I said at the end of chapter 6, by the end of my time as an independent financial advisor, I was over it. Clients are never or rarely happy. I mean, I get it, of course, but I was getting calls day and night, to say nothing of the rigors of managing many portfolios at once. Clients would be calling in all irritated if their stocks weren't making as much money as everyone else's, if they're making some money but not as much as they wanted to make, or they were just kind of stagnant and not really making or losing money; so no matter what, people just tended to be upset. Not every client, mind you; I did have some great ones as well.

I mean, money is THE stressor for the modern man. More than half of all divorces cite money or disagreements over finances as the primary factor for the failure, which I personally can't understand but saw with my own eyes. Many times, I felt like I was a counselor with my married clients. They would sit in my office during a portfolio review and start arguing right in front of me, which of course, was awkward, to say the least. Ultimately, I would end up giving more marital advice than financial. My wife and I have a policy when it comes to money: it's just money; we'll make more! Granted, we do believe in saving and budgeting, but we've never argued over money, and I'm near certain we never will.

105

The problem is when money becomes a preoccupation in and of itself; you know, "for the love of money," the amassing of wealth with no real goal or just the goal of having a lot of money to the point of obsession. I've dealt with these types, and it's not the kind of person I could be friends with. Making money isn't a good or bad thing. At least it shouldn't be. It's a means to an end. That's why it's important to have financial goals—know what you are working toward to know sanctification.

At this point, I had met all the objectives in the financial advisory world, which defined my happiness. I'd met my goals and then some.

I had a nice house, motorcycle, and car. I had found love, which I was not looking for but now couldn't imagine being without. As you might imagine, by this point, I had been practicing what I was preaching for a while, so we were not just financially stable but felt a bit of security. Then again, is there really any such thing as security? As far as Maslow's Hierarchy of Needs is concerned, I was supposed to feel self-actualized: needs met, wants met, even squishy and subtle desires achieved. But I was nonetheless gripped with dissatisfaction.

Bored? Sure, I had been herding cats for quite a while now, and the grind was wearing on me, but it was definitely more of a lack of fulfillment. I was satisfied with a job well done, but the tasks were no longer giving me the level of joy I had come to expect from life. When you get used to setting goals and meeting them, one of the possible side-effects is a restless spirit! Of course, I've always been cursed and blessed with an insatiable curiosity, so it was with only a little trepidation, a big word for a little fear, that I came home one day and looked at my wife.

"Angie, you know, I'm just not getting any satisfaction out of being a stockbroker anymore." We talked and talked over a period of time and then talked about it some more.

"You know what I loved about all the jobs I've had?" I said one time. "It's teaching people how to do things. Training."

I took a look at the idea and started doing research; although I love all things motivational, I honestly wasn't sure I was able to start making a living at motivational speaking. The truth is that, ultimately, public speaking was a goal in life, but I figured I'd need to gray up the hair a little bit first and get a little more wisdom. So, to that end, I landed on the idea of training folks that want to become financial advisors and insurance agents.

After doing more research, my wife and I bought AD Banker & Company, a franchise out of Kansas. We purchased the franchise territory of North Carolina along with it, so it was named AD Banker of North Carolina. This is what gave us the right to train people for the tests required to sell insurance: life and health, property, and casualty, as well as securities licensing for the Series 6, 65, Series 7, and any other securities licensing courses we could.

At first, AD Banker of North Carolina started out with just a website, only offering online classes. People would purchase the courses, take tests, and receive certificates. And as I said, we were doing everything remotely. Angie did all of the marketing, contacted the different insurance and financial firms, and solicited new business with our company and website. Before we knew it, we had started growing at a pretty good pace, and pretty soon, we needed to begin searching for office and classroom space.

If you've never leased commercial space, it can be pretty intimidating. I mean, I had no real idea of what I could negotiate on or what the leasing terms should be. Although we had a real estate agent, quite honestly, they worked for the REIT (Real Estate Investment Trust), leasing the property; therefore, I'm pretty sure they had the property's best interest at heart. I'm not saying that they were out to screw us, but we could have gotten a better deal had we hired someone to represent us solely.

After a month or so of searching, we landed on a perfect location in a beautiful high-rise building in Cary, NC, that had everything that we needed. It was a nice space with a good-sized waiting area, common area, restroom, an office for me as Angie worked out of the home, and a conference room area so large that we could set it up for a classroom big enough to hold twenty people. It had a lot of modern finishes like a ceiling-mounted projector and wall-mounted screens for my PowerPoint presentations. We bought really nice tables and chairs for the students. Once the office was completely decorated and furnished, we were ready to start advertising!

I was excited and a bit nervous all at the same time. Not really to the point that I thought that maybe I had *bitten off more than I could chew* nervous, but I guess I was worried about spending all this money and no one showing up for the training. And what if I sucked at this new venture? I mean, I knew HOW to sell investments and advise folks, but training someone on what they needed to know to obtain the license is quite honestly a different animal altogether.

I had the study guides from our main franchise office and had spent a week in Overland Park, Kansas, at the home office learning different teaching techniques and how to train people to pass an exam. It's interesting to note that although I have spent many hours of my life on an actual stage in front of sometimes hundreds of people, I was still nervous at the prospect of standing in front of a group of strangers with no more than twenty people at a time. It was probably the added pressure of being responsible for helping them pass an exam that could change their lives! And when I say "change their lives," there are people I have trained back then who are now making upwards of half a million dollars or more a year! Now you can't make a living on that, but it's an excellent start! Okay, that's a joke I heard at a seminar once and use it every chance I can.

Angie is now setting people up for in-person training. We set up a schedule to hold two-day classes once a week, and each one was usually on a different license type. For example, life and health one week, property and casualty the next, and then a class on passing the Series 6, 65, 7, and so on. The good news is we could obviously charge more for in-person classes, so our revenue started to climb, which is important because we had bills to pay, like most folks. It didn't take long before our classes started filling up, and we realized that we might need a larger classroom! We kept that office and small classroom for a while as we had a lease on it, but as our classes grew, we started renting out different hotel rooms to conduct the training. At one point, we had some classes with as many as one hundred people in the room. Crazy! And let me just say, do you have any idea how tough it is to field questions from a hundred people? The truth is that's too large of a "classroom," but the demand was pretty high, and I knew I had the capability and skillset to deliver the training effectively.

True, I did some instruction while stationed at the RIP and taught Rangers to work as a cohesive team and how to operate in any given scenario. However, stepping into the role of a more formal educator, standing at the front of a room wearing a nice suit (I clean up nicely), and actively teaching gave me a sense of professional satisfaction that I had not felt in years.

This was a good, no, a *great* feeling. Again, I'm satisfying my ego by getting in front of a crowd and performing, if you will, which gives me great joy. My wife and I would operate AD Banker of North Carolina for a little more than three years, and it was giving me that feeling of badassdom in a totally different way. There was no blood, sweat, or tears this time but a nice warm glow. No blisters, bruises, or exhaustion for this feeling—I was teaching others how to succeed and become a badass in their own right! I had my piece of the pie—I do like pie—and I was showing others how to grab theirs too. It was clear now that I had found what I wanted to do with myself. I knew that I wanted to be in front of audiences and train, teach, mentor, motivate, and strive to leave them better off than how I found them!

Rolling my love of the stage together with my headstrong, can-do attitude and what I learned about instruction and demonstration from the Rangers, I wanted to be a Tony Robbins and Eddie Van Halen clone, the Schwarzenegger of Speaking, the Maverick of Motivation! I was inciting a *Quiet Riot* in the hearts of young men and women, and I loved it.

What I didn't love were the corporate masters, who actually owned the franchise, breathing down my neck. Sadly, it was owned by a family, and like most families, there is usually some tension that trickles down to affect everyone working for them. It was like the clients I managed portfolios for all over again! No one thing, just a little lack of faith in who was running the show. It was a brother-sister pair that were in charge and, I don't know, I just think there were some problems with the company. At one point, the brother left the business, and amidst our growing indecision, we decided to sell it off as we felt it was headed south.

111

It was definitely the turning point for me.

I loved teaching; I loved instruction; I loved the life! In fact, by the last year we were doing it, I was on the road several days a week doing eight-hour seminars. It really made me happy when I would get e-mails from people saying, "Hey, thank you, I would listen to Michael teach a class on paint drying for eight hours." It was good to get affirmation that I was on the right path. When you're rocking out on stage or training in the military, you get instant feedback and know immediately if you're doing good or not. In the business world, it can be hard to know without feedback.

It all came down to *making a difference* for me; the stage, the money, and the dynamic environment were great, but it was knowing I was changing lives that really gave me the sense of satisfaction I was looking for. With a newfound love of instruction and teaching, we sold AD Banker, but now I didn't know what I wanted to be when I grew up!

Listen to me: you MUST go for your dreams, as cliché as that may sound! Some of you might be thinking that buying AD Banker turned out bad because we ultimately sold it, and we didn't get "rich." What you need to really grasp is that with chasing your purpose, discovering your God-given gifts, and going after your dreams, you have to step out on faith and do that thing that keeps you up at night! It's nagging at you right now. It's right there in your head, tapping on your forehead from the inside, screaming, "Let me out!"

Yes, that *did* sound like a line from a Stephen King book, I know, but I'm praying that I'm getting my point across.

The last time I checked, time wasn't waiting on any of us, so
"Get busy living or get busy dying" (*The Shawshank Redemption*).

CHAPTER 9: "BODIES"

Drowning Pool; 2001

Speak What You Want into Existence

I remember driving around one afternoon in Cary and came across this gym called LA Boxing. It was closed at the time, and I could see through the large glass windows boxing heavy bags hanging, like twenty or more of them in a type of cage. Intrigued, I parked, got out, and started looking into the windows around the gym. A large boxing ring stood about four feet off the floor, surrounded by some weight equipment, jump ropes, etc. The colors were mostly black and red, and quite honestly, it was the most incredible gym I'd ever seen. After getting back home, I immediately got on the internet and researched the gym and the industry as a whole: fitness boxing and kickboxing. It turned out that it was all the rage, as they say, and like so many, martial arts had started in California. Well, LA Boxing began in California, but there were plenty of boxing/ kickboxing gyms across the country that I didn't even know existed until now.

The UFC (Ultimate Fighting Championship) was getting really big at the time, still is, for that matter. The official UFC Gym was huge: thirty thousand square feet on average, with boxing, kickboxing, and an MMA ring that was out in LA, but it wasn't franchising at the time. There were companies like CKO on the eastern seaboard and TITLE Boxing Club, which is still a popular and successful gym to this day. TITLE Boxing equipment, gloves, bags, etc., has been a brand for decades.

Interestingly, most folks don't know that boxing and kickboxing workouts burn a LOT of calories. I would venture to say it's one of the top three workouts that you could do. Cycling and swimming are also at the top. As a matter of fact, as I ventured into the world of fitness boxing, I would routinely burn eight hundred to one thousand calories in one hour! Hard to believe, maybe, and you do have to put the energy into the workout. Not to mention that boxing is one of the original HIIT workouts: high-intensity interval training.

The short version is doing something with high intensity for a period of time and then slowing down for the purpose of dropping the heart rate for a short period and then BAM! Back up again! You are to do this for the most part until you physically can't do the exercise anymore. It's like doing bicep curls for the heart. Since you can't isolate the heart like you can the bicep when exercising, HIIT training is the best way to simulate the contracting and releasing of the heart muscle. Not to mention the fact that your oxygen consumption rate increases much more rapidly than just doing steady-state cardio (running at the same pace for a long distance, for example). I always tell folks if they are going to run on a treadmill, don't just run at the same pace for thirty minutes. Sprint as fast as you can for a minute and jog for two minutes. I promise you that you'll feel a huge difference, and you'll burn way more calories!

Now, I need to be clear that I'm not "really" a boxer; at least, I don't want to put myself in the same category as those that have mastered the skills of "the sweet science." The term "sweet science" comes from British sportswriter Pierce Egan, an avid follower of the prizefighting scene in the early 1800s. I did box for a short time during my first enlistment in the 82d and spent a period on TDY (Temporary Duty) boxing for the post. These are three round bouts wearing headgear and are scored with points based on landing punches. It's quite a difficult task to knock someone out in three rounds wearing the headgear for well-trained boxers, and the truth is that I've never really been that good at the sport. I just liked it as it gave me a sense of empowerment. Remember, I was bullied quite a bit in school because I was a small dude. Well, guess what, some of the smallest men on the planet have turned out to be some of the greatest fighters—in and out of the ring!

Since I was casting around for a new stimulating venture, I realized that since I used to do some boxing, had a background in military hand-to-hand training, was into health and fitness, and I was newly intrigued with fitness boxing, then I might give it a go. I have to admit, however, popular as it was, and even though some franchises were doing pretty well, we had just gotten out of a franchise relationship. The constraints of working under someone else's business model weren't something either my wife or I wanted.

It was time to return to being my own boss.

My wife and I hit the drawing board and started researching what it takes to open and run a gym. Specifically, a boxing/kickboxing gym. After a month or so, we developed a business plan and started putting the wheels in motion to open the gym with a great deal of excitement. But what do we call it? A name is extremely important, as it needs to pull people in. It needed to sound badass and professional at the same time. But most of all, it needed to tell people what we do! After going through what seemed like a thousand names, we landed on the name: East Coast Boxing.

Now, I say, "Speak what you want into existence" because right when we were only a few days from signing the paperwork on the lease for the gym, we were still about $75,000 short! I mean, we were all set up for the most part, had T-shirts made, a Facebook page launched that was growing in popularity, and of course, we had already spent some initial outlay of cash, but we still needed a good chunk of change to finish the build-out and get started. You see, as much as you may think that just because you have a great business idea that banks will just throw money at you, that's sadly not true in the least. I had pitched my idea over a couple of months, all ending in closed doors. And even though I felt now and then that we were heading down a dead-end road, my wife and I kept talking about it, praying about it; we stayed positive and kept moving forward *as if.*

I've ALWAYS believed in speaking what you want into existence! I have done this many times in my life, so I know with all my heart and soul that it absolutely works! In

118

the end, just a few days before we were scheduled to sign the lease, the money came in! And while I can't go into the details of the deal because it's a personal thing, let's just say an angel put the money in our hands. This dream would never have come together had we given up, stopped striving, and not talked about it "AS IF" it already existed.

Once we were up and running, I would say that paying the money back was like the proverbial monkey on my back. I worked like a dog and did what I could to put money aside. I'm proud to say that we paid the loan back in less than a year, and to this day, I'm forever grateful to the source of the loan.

I've always been a believer in speaking what you want into existence. State your intentions. Remain positive, expect the best, take ACTION, and you'll be surprised how often you'll accomplish your goals. Sure, failures happen, but the real winners in life are the ones who understand that when you get knocked down, you get up and keep moving forward. As long as you're not all show and no go, talking about your needs and desires with the people around you will help motivate and keep you on track. Sharing your ideas, two-way communication, and honesty is the only way you're ever going to learn, grow, and sometimes come across an unexpected windfall from a surprising source.

We grew ECB into a major powerhouse gym! Our membership grew every month, and our members became these champions of the brand, ECB. Our logo was branded onto shirts and gear, and it sold out off our shelves weekly.

119

We had some of the toughest trainers in the industry, and I know that most gym owners will say the same, but I'm telling you, the reputation that ECB had was, "They will literally kick your ass into shape!" I came to find that many people in the community wouldn't join the gym because they were afraid.

Mind you, we were not a full-contact gym for the average member, strictly fitness classes and one-on-one personal training. So I'm not sure why people were afraid except for the fact that some folks would throw up in class or even pass out, and then there was the occasional ambulance call. Yes, waivers were signed, first aid measures were in place, and all staff were certified personal trainers and certified in CPR. So, there's that.

All I'm trying to say is that East Coast Boxing wasn't for the faint of heart. I'm not kidding; like, you needed a doctor's clearance to be a member. It was for no excuse-making, no-holds-barred, ready-to-sweat-like-a-pig, bag-smashing, burpee-loving, combo-throwing freaks! (They weren't afraid to bleed either.)

No different than losing weight and getting into great shape, it's important to always be taking steps toward your goal, long, leaping strides if you can, or tiny incremental ones when the going gets tough. Dreams don't achieve themselves and almost never in a vacuum. Your brain's basically a computer in a certain fashion. What you say comes out of your mouth but goes right back into your ears.

You hear it, and your brain begins making the necessary plans for you to take action and to make it come true.

Now, as I said, you must take ACTION. If I hadn't been calling vendors looking for the gym equipment we needed or marketing items and saying, "Hey, make that logo, we're going to need that!" it wouldn't have come together. Like any "overnight success," what people saw was not only the result of months and months of hard work, but the net sum of my entire life up to this point.

You know it's interesting to point out that when you start something and start achieving any type of success, you'll find that some folks will begin to judge you. Sadly, sometimes these folks are friends or family, but your employees will do this as well. Not all; some are incredibly dedicated to your success, but there are others that will talk behind your back and tell others that you're getting rich from their hard work, and before you know it, some are demanding higher wages. Those folks? I sent packing right out the front door. The truth is that most businesses, ECB notwithstanding, don't even turn a profit for the first five years. It's true that we had money coming in from the memberships and personal training sales, but the overhead was over $16,000 a month before Angie and I made one dollar of profit. And even in the months that we made more than $16,000, we would take any profits and put it right back into the business.

We were the sponsor for a popular local morning radio show, *Bob and the Showgram*, for the first couple of years that we were open. We ran twenty-plus ads a week, and I would go in once a month and do a promo spot talking with the host, Bob Dumas, for fifteen to twenty minutes. Ultimately, the entire on-air *Showgram* staff (all four of them!) joined East Coast Boxing. As you could imagine, advertising isn't cheap, but a business that doesn't advertise doesn't stay in business very long.

Over the years of my life, I have learned how to push myself: my mind and body in the army, commanding the attention of an audience as a rocker, teaching complex concepts to a crowd in AD Banker, and balancing a spreadsheet as a stockbroker and financial advisor. This was my life's work, a culmination of all my skills. But it never would have happened if I had not woken up every day with a positive attitude and set those pieces into motion, keeping them moving, and then pushed those sons of bitches when they stalled.

You cannot let up!

Make "This is going to happen" your train of thought instead of "Wouldn't it be great if this happened?"

We had a poster on the wall at East Coast Boxing, and it said this:

WHILE AT EAST COAST BOXING . . .

CRAWLING IS ACCEPTABLE

FALLING IS ACCEPTABLE

PUKING IS ACCEPTABLE

CRYING IS ACCEPTABLE

BLOOD IS ACCEPTABLE

PAIN IS ACCEPTABLE

QUITTING IS NOT.

We ran East Coast Boxing for a few years, and I loved every minute of it for the most part. I say for the most part because no matter what you do in this lifetime, conflict and drama will be there. As long as people work together and there's a chain of command, there will be drama. As long as there's jealousy and greed, there will be conflict. Bottom line: there will always be drama. These steal joy, so be careful not to let it get the best of you!

In the meantime, competition surrounding the gym got pretty fierce. It's like as soon as a shiny new object is dangled in front of people, they tend to want to chase after it and try the next best thing. We didn't really suffer from this as. By this point, we had a pretty solid membership base that was incredibly dedicated to ECB. There's always a danger when you catch a trend. The number of high-impact exercise options in our area exploded. Not just other MMA-type studios but CrossFit, traditional weightlifting gyms, and circuit training studios all sprung up around us like toadstools after a rain. We struggled a bit at first, but we survived. Angie and I tossed around the idea of starting a franchise, but in the end, we discarded that idea for a multitude of reasons that are too boring to read about, I assure you. Having been franchisees ourselves, perhaps we were just sour on the whole idea.

We had that thing happen where we both sort of woke up one morning and decided we didn't want this to be the rest of our lives.

I still had it in my mind that I wanted to do public speaking, even when I was teaching the fine art of smashing heads, er —I mean, heavy bags. I was invited to be a keynote speaker for the company that ran our gym's computer software. The company is called Mindbody; their offices are in California, and they wanted me to come out and speak at a very large convention. I had done seminars on my proprietary "reverse sales process" in the past (I have a podcast episode about it), but I passed at the time due to some conflicts. I regret it now, but it reminded me that public speaking, motivational speaking, and leading seminars like that were an option in my future. You know: being a rock star!

I wanted to be on stage. I wanted to inspire and motivate, to mentor and help people.

CHAPTER 10: "IT'S A LONG WAY TO THE TOP"

AC/DC, 1975

Keep on Facing the Fear; Keep on Growing

After we sold East Coast Boxing and walked away from that, which I covered in the previous chapter, I wasn't really sure what I wanted to do next.

While I did do some consulting with the gym that I sold East Coast Boxing to, I was only spending a few hours a week doing that. Most of the time, I was at home with Angie helping run her business. And I got a great deal of satisfaction from that. She had been my wingman for so long it was great being able to return the favor.

But ultimately, I guess, I needed to figure out what I wanted to do now.

Remember, I always knew what I wanted to do: all the way back when I was a boy (chapter one), where I got that guitar, and I wanted to be a rockstar. And none of that ever sounded crazy to me, but I guess that's because I knew it was possible—I'd toured, gone wild on stage, and hyped a crowd. But I don't know. I believe most people want to be a rock star in some form or fashion.

125

If you don't believe me, just look at Instagram, Facebook, TikTok, and all the rest; we live in a society where everybody wants to get those "likes." We want to get someone double tapping our Instagram picture. Everyone is looking for their fifteen minutes of fame. We want followers on TikTok and friends on Facebook. Most people I know get a kick out of more people joining their page, except maybe my wife. She truly does not seek fame and fortune.

But most want the limelight. We want people looking at us. I can't explain why, but the first time I strapped a guitar around my neck and got on stage in front of a bunch of people, I loved it. I loved the feeling that it gave me as I went into the army and was promoted rather quickly and became a sergeant. I was put in charge of troops, and that was my first taste of leadership. No call-and-response with a crowd ever gave me the thrill of leading a unit of badass military personnel.

I loved being a rocker, though. When I got out of the army the first time, I moved to Florida and started playing in a band; I was actually a professional musician being *paid* to get on stage to wail, scream, and jump. That feeling of being a real rock star, of course, on a much smaller level, is the feeling of making a great night for people, the feeling of changing up a room and getting charged up. Not to the point of, you know, Led Zeppelin or any of the international bands, but we rocked hundreds. Our biggest shows were maybe a few thousand. Nonetheless, I got to experience being on stage in front of teeming masses of unruly people, hearing people scream, clap, and cheer night after night.

This was the feeling that I was always looking for: to make people feel good.

But the truth is I thought it was because I wanted to be a performer. A little later and a little wiser, I'd learn it wasn't so much being a performer. Mostly, it was that immediate satisfaction of how people felt when I was in front of them doing something that made them feel good in this case, if not playing music, singing, and entertaining in general.

It was just the most fantastic experience of my life. Like I mentioned in previous chapters, it's not that I couldn't handle playing music and, you know, the proverbial "sex, drugs, and rock 'n' roll." It was just, in my core, being a rock star and pursuing that lifestyle wasn't what I *really* wanted. It was a means to an end. I knew I needed *something* to fulfill my soul in the whole wanting-to-entertain-people thing.

And as cliché as this may sound, I did want to help people. I do want to make your lives better.

I left the band knowing that cocaine and late nights, living a life of semi-debauchery, wasn't *really* what my future was supposed to hold. I quit and walked out the door. Some of the best memories of my life will be playing in that band. I made great friends, made mistakes along the way, and many times, I screwed up. I probably wasn't the best person that I could have been at that time. I think that's why I knew I had to go back to the army.

127

It was the best decision I could've made, in hindsight.

I reenlisted and started my now second tour of duty; went back in, signed up for a ranger contract, and somehow made it through the indoctrination program, through the pre-ranger program, and through ranger school itself. I pinned the proverbial black-and-gold Ranger Tab on for real.

One of the most significant accomplishments of my life to date was when my dad pinned that tab on, and I'll never forget it as long as I live.

I started serving in the RIP, which is part of the regimental headquarters for the ranger unit. I'm not going to rehash everything again (chapter four), but I was living my best life. And in a way, it was fulfilling again. This idea of being a rock star proved to be conceptual; it wasn't the rocking that I loved but the inspiring, even leading.

Side note: Back then, the Rangers exclusively wore the black beret—the undisputed (okay . . . all other special ops units will dispute that) badasses of the entire armed forces. Nowadays, all soldiers wear black berets. But I don't want to get into that because, quite frankly, it irritates me just a little bit because the black beret *used to be* awarded to the Rangers because of their specialty in night operations. The black beret was something of significance. It was something that truly meant that you were an elite soldier.

I mean, just read the ranger creed. I'm not going to recite it to you, but I included it at the very end: being a ranger meant that I was an elite soldier. And I was proud of that distinction because it was something not everyone could accomplish. This is not to sound arrogant; I think everybody reading this needs to understand that everyone probably has a personality trait they are really proud of, and everybody has different goals in life. Some of you reading this may have no desire to be a rock star, but everyone wants to shine at what they do. You may have no desire to stand in front of crowds. You may have no desire whatsoever to seek any kind of fame, and that's okay. I think, however, that everyone wants acceptance, that most folks inherently want to genuinely help people.

At least that's what I pray. I'd hate to think that this world is just, I don't know, a bunch of evil and hatred-filled people barely hiding their rage. I know it's not, though the Information Age's double-edged sword has seemingly given a louder voice to the ignorant and angry than to the kind and intelligent.

You know you can't have evil without good. I believe, still, that there is way more good than evil in the world—and I have seen evil. I mean, it's evident every day in the news, but I do think good overall prevails in our society; you have to remember that since "if it bleeds, it leads" is true for the media, you're only ever going to see bad news reported.

So, the point I'm getting to is that I have now completed almost fifteen years in the United States Army. I did not retire, and people ask me all the time, "Why didn't you retire?" and I don't really have a great answer for that. The DA wanted me to go overseas on another tour. I was a recruiter at that time, and they asked me to go abroad for my next tour, or I could reenlist and became a full-time recruiter.

The short story is I just didn't want that in life. At that point, I knew there was something more significant than I wanted to pursue. I am very proud of my military service. I'm very proud that I served in the army. I'm proud of everything that I have accomplished while serving my country.

Still, I walked out, which is not something that most E-7's do!

An E-7 is a sergeant first class in the army. Walking away is something that most senior Non-Commissioned Officers just don't do. I had a one-star general call me one day.

"What the hell do you think you're doing? Senior NCOs don't walk out of the army five years before retirement!"

"This one does!"

Because, quite frankly, I'm employable. I had options. There are things I could do. And it's not a big deal; I'm very proud that I served, but at the end of the day, retirement income from the military did not provide the living that I was looking for. It's nice to have, and God bless every retired veteran out there that's served in any branch of the armed forces as they are truly the greatest people on the plane. That doesn't mean you had to have served to be a great person, but I have nothing but the utmost respect for anyone that served in any branch of the armed forces. I don't care if it was two years, five years, ten years, or you served a whole career, and it's been your life.

So, I walked away and didn't know what I was going to do at that point. After going through everything I covered in earlier chapters, ultimately, I was a salesperson, and I was, if I may, very good at it. I moved through the phase of being a stockbroker, and after many years doing that, it wasn't giving me personal satisfaction anymore; the thrill of living I had come to expect from my days was bland again. The job just wasn't dynamic enough, the demands of the clients too unrelenting.

Angie and I, as mentioned earlier, opened a franchise called AD Banker of North Carolina. That was the business where we trained people to become financial advisors, insurance agents, stockbrokers, and whatever license that they needed. I was also conducting sales training. Just because you studied to get a stockbroker license doesn't mean they teach you how to be a great salesperson—getting an insurance license doesn't magically teach you how to sell insurance. Being a financial advisor is only about 10 percent of the job at the end of the day. Ninety percent of the job is prospecting and getting in front of people, selling them on using your services, and financial investment in general. If you're not a good salesperson, you are not going to get the business you need or make a living.

All too often, many of these companies out here spend way too much time focusing on the wrong things. I filled that education gap for many years. My awesome wife would work out of the house and set me up for these training seminars with all these different companies. I mean, she is really the brains behind anything we've ever done. We truly are a great team. Anyway, she would set me up to go do the training, and I would spend many days of the week on the road out doing the speaking engagements. That ultimately burned me out because I was spending a LOT of time on the road.

After eight hours leading a workshop running my mouth, I didn't want to speak to anybody for the rest of the day! Speaking long hours can be pretty harsh on the vocal cords. So, of course, as you've already read, after AD Banker, I decided to go a completely different route. So we spoke East Coast Boxing into existence; again, not to rehash the entire chapter, but just to give you a little reminder.

I've always loved boxing but was never really good at it, to be truthful. Quite frankly, I kind of sucked at it, but I loved it! It's also one of the most incredible ways to get in shape. It's the absolute perfect HIIT training. HIIT means high-intensity interval training, and if you research that, it simply means doing something that's going to elevate the heart rate for a period of time, then lower the heart rate for a longer period of time, and then you do it again. So in boxing, if you think about it, you're doing three minutes on in the ring and then one minute off, taking a break. Then three minutes on again, then one minute off, three minutes on, one minute off, and so on.

You can't exercise the heart directly; that's why I've never been a fan of steady-state cardio. I don't believe in running the heart to the red line. That's not good for a car's engine, and the last time I checked, the heart IS the engine in the body. Raising the heart rate for a short period of time and then lowering the heart rate back down; that's the key. It's kind of like doing bicep curls. You raise the dumbbells, squeeze the bicep, and when you release, raise the dumbbell, squeeze the bicep, and then you release. This is the only way to target the bicep. When doing HIIT training, you're elevating the heart rate, squeezing the heart muscle, and then releasing. You repeat that over and over again, therefore, strengthening the heart and whatever you're working on at the same time.

We had a good run with East Coast Boxing. I truly loved it and loved helping people! I still think about it today: reopening ECB and taking it to a whole other level!

But that remains to be seen.

Moving along, after we sold off ECB, I sat at home, literally, for a couple of years, not really knowing which route I was going to take. I knew I still wanted to be a rock star. I knew I loved speaking to audiences and, you know, kind of wanted to be a motivational speaker. But you don't really just think that one and wake up saying, "I'm going to be a motivational speaker!" and just become one. I know Tony Robbins did exactly that, and he crushed it. He did great at it. Maybe that was his true calling, and he was fortunate enough to find it at such an early age.

Also, maybe it was my lack of belief in myself, as much as I preach believing in myself, that I didn't think I could be a motivational speaker. As I'm getting older now, and a little bit more gray is starting to creep into my beard, and I've been through quite a bit; maybe I'm ready. It's possible nobody would have been inspired had I tried this path before proving myself in so many different fields. I haven't told you everything that I've been through in this book, just a small snapshot of what I've done in my lifetime. But I figured I was getting closer to ultimately doing what I felt I was called to do, which is to be a speaker. An inspirational speaker. A motivational speaker on a stage in front of people for the purpose of helping.

The truth is over a couple of years of sitting around, I'm here to tell you that it is not good for anyone.

You know, the whole idle mind saying; the devil loves an idle mind, and you should not sit around. Left to your own devices, you can get in trouble. I'm not saying I'm out doing stuff to get in trouble. I'm just saying I'm not thinking at my fullest capability or living up to my expectations for myself. I was sitting around and trying to figure out what to do. By doing so, I let us get into a little bit of a financial bind. Not bankruptcy or risking my family living in the streets. We're not standing on the edge of a precipice looking down into the abyss, but we'd spent money that had been put aside for the future.

So I knew I had to do something; I didn't want a normal job, but I started working at this store called Sam Ash, which is a very large music store up and down the eastern seaboard. They sell music gear, instruments, and pro audio equipment; remember, I play guitar. So, I thought that'd be kind of a cool thing to do while I was figuring out my next step in life. I would sell guitars. At this time, I had a ponytail, large gauges in my ears, and I was covered in tattoos. If you haven't seen a picture of me, I look like a rock star.

I walked in the door, filled out an application, and applied for the job. Low and behold, they hired me. Now I read the payment plan they hired me under, and the truth is it sucked. I stepped into the company, which maybe had about twenty salespeople, and it only took me a few weeks to work my way up to number three. Not number two; not number one; but number three. Now, having read this far, you may ask yourself, why didn't I make it to number one? That's because the two guys that were at number one and number two were always jockeying for those positions each month and had been in the business for fifteen to twenty years. They had a book of sales and repeat referrals coming in the door asking for them by name. Every time you sell a piece of equipment from a music store, you get paid a commission, and those guys had it down to an art.

There's a small hourly wage that you get paid, but otherwise, it's a commission job. These guys just had a huge collection of customers that I just couldn't compete with. There were areas that I *could* compete with and sold extended warranties on products and things like that, so I did hit number one in other areas, but, in all fairness, these guys were killers and genuinely great at what they did, as well as being great people. I just couldn't beat them. I would have needed a lot more tenure on the job if I ever planned on hitting their numbers. Although I loved working at the store, loved selling pro audio equipment, and loved selling guitars, it was the people I worked with that really made that job. These were all musicians, my people; musicians are nuts! With all the love in my heart, I say that it was just a great place to work.

However, there's no real money in it.

The pay plan, quite frankly, was not good. I don't know whether or not there's a lot of profit in music equipment because I never researched it enough. I just know what the company paid me. I could sell a $3,000 public address system, and I'd make $15. Trust me, that's not a very good commission plan. In all fairness, I don't know what the cost was for the company, so I'm just giving my opinion. I didn't get to see the internal numbers. I'm an adult, I accepted the pay plan, and that's just what it was. After paying for insurance, because my family needs health insurance, and Uncle Sam gets his less-than-a-fair share, I would get my paycheck and what was left of it was always a little disheartening considering what I was used to. I ended up clearing only a few hundred dollars a week!

Luckily, Angie was running her business at home too, and that definitely helped support us. But there comes the point where you're putting in forty to fifty hours a week and working Saturdays and Sundays too. If you're working those kinds of hours, you want to think that you'll make more money than just a few hundred dollars after all is said and done. I had made the decision to leave, but I almost stayed for $500 a week! They actually offered me a guarantee of $500 a week plus commission if I stayed and did not leave the company.

I hate to admit it, but in a moment of weakness, I came home and was talking to Angie that night and thought maybe I should stay? I ended up not taking the offer because, at the same time, I was talking to someone at a car dealership that I had bought a car from years ago. The car lot messaged me and said they were opening up this new dealership in Apex, where I lived.

And they said, you know, I'd be really good at selling cars.

I have spent my life making fun of used car salespeople—I surely wasn't going to become one! I mean, that's not really true; I haven't spent my life making fun of used car salespeople. But you know that used car salespeople are definitely the brunt of a lot of jokes and probably not the most respected people on the planet, which is too bad. Since I've been in the car business, I've met some really great people. It took me a couple of months to go in and talk to this gentleman by the name of Dory.

I finally did go down there; I interviewed with Dory, and he offered me the job. You should know that even after offering me the job, I wasn't sure it was something I wanted to do. This is not really who I am—or so I thought. I'm more of a start-my-own company, do-my-own-thing kind of a guy. Hell, I don't even like working for people. But I don't know; something was resonating with me about this. Maybe he sold me on it! And you know, my wife, who is always a source of great inspiration for me (because I mean, she is my partner, my wife, my everything), she said, "You know, maybe it's something you should do."

My dad even told me all my life that I should sell cars.

So, I thought, you know what? I'm going to go for it. I took the job, and I went to work.

At the time, the company was called Hanna Imports of Apex. It's now just Apex Imports but the same company. I went to work in December of 2016 as a car salesman on the lot. Selling cars, as it turned out, was something I was pretty good at.

In my first month, I sold a lot of cars, and in my second month and third month too. Because I was posting how many cars I had sold on social media, it was getting the attention of other car dealerships in the area. A friend of mine, who had worked at a major dealership for thirty-eight years at the time, called me one day and said, "Are you really selling that many cars?"

"Yes," I said. "I'm really selling that many cars. It really isn't that difficult."

"You're not meant to sell cars, man! You're meant to manage those that do! You need to be a sales manager or a finance manager. You have too much experience in the world of sales to be running that parking lot and moving metal."

They offered me a job, and the truth is I took it. But when I put in my two weeks' notice to my general manager, who is a good friend of mine to this day, he said, "You know, I really don't want to lose ya, but I totally understand you want to seek better opportunities."

I explained to him how much I appreciated everything. The fact that he hired a guy with a neck tattoo, ponytail, and big holes in his ears, he took a chance with me, and I did appreciate that. I believe that we are supposed to be honorable to those that employ us and be dedicated. I felt guilty, but my income objectives had changed. Since it turned out I was really good at this car selling thing, and we were in a lurch, I owed it to our family's bottom line to keep moving up.

I put in two weeks' notice and didn't let up selling in the meantime; I came to work every day and sold like a madman. One night, the owner came in and said I need to speak to you in my office. I walked in and sat down with him.

"You know, I honestly think you should stay here at the dealership because you have a lifetime of selling experience, and we'd like to keep you on."
He offered me a floor closer position, which was not part of their business model at the time. A floor closer is nothing more than someone that stays on the sales floor, and as a salesperson is trying to close a deal on selling a car, the "closer" comes in and, basically, seals the deal. I was basically a closer already and was doing it month after month anyway.

So I *accepted* the position and called up the other company and said I was sorry, I know I said I would come work for you, and I feel guilty about that.

Sometimes in life, you do have to do what's best for you, and I wanted to see this new dealership through. I wanted to see the growth of it and be part of it. I felt invested. And the fact they were offering me a management position and to create a whole new role just to keep me resonated with me because it's a perfect fit for who I am. It's what I do.

Month after month after month, I put in the hours and spent my days and nights closing deals.

Here's a valuable lesson that I want to get across before I finish up. Right at the six-month point of being the floor closer, I wasn't making great money, but I was making good money. I was making a lot more than I was making working at Sam Ash, for sure. One night, I came home, and I'm talking to my wife, and she says, "So, how long do you think you'll be a floor closer before they make you a sales manager and put you on the sales desk?"

"I don't know; it could be another six months or two years because we currently have two sales managers. That's the only management position they have. They're not going to put a third sales manager on the desk. The two sales managers we have, who knows how long they'll be in these positions? It doesn't look like they're going to quit anytime soon. So, I don't know."

"Do you love the job?" she asked.

"I do. I enjoy it. I get satisfaction from doing so."

That seems to be key to doing something meaningful in life. Do you get satisfaction from your job? Do you even enjoy it?

I did; I do.

I went to work the next day. It was a Friday, and I remembered doing my job with one of the sales managers, Brian. He was a great guy, and everybody loved him; a great sales manager who did his job well. So there was no reason to believe that Brian would ever leave the dealership anytime soon. As fate would have it, at two o'clock in the afternoon, I walked up to the sales desk, and a good friend of mine by the name of Rick, he was the other sales manager at the time, looked at me and said, "Brian's gone."

I was like, "What do you mean Brian's gone?"

"Well, he quit."

"Brian quit. No way!"

I walked around and sat down in Brian's chair and looked around at the desk.

"Look! All his stuff is gone!" Rick pointed out.

Sure enough, everything he had here, his pins and pictures, stuff on the desk, were all gone.

"So, what happened?"

"Nothing. He just decided that he was going to open his own car business, so he walked into Dory's office, said 'I'm opening my own business. I'm putting in my two weeks' notice.'"

Dory just told him, "Look, if you need to go, go ahead and go; we wish you all the best."

Shocked by this, I'm sitting there in Brian's old chair behind the sales desk. About that time, Dory walks into the room. Remember, he's the general manager, so he walks around the corner, and I'm sitting in the big chair. I turned around and looked at him, and I said, boldly (perhaps in hindsight a little too boldly), "This is now my job."

Of course, he *could* have just kicked me out of the chair and said, "Get back on the floor and do your job."

But he didn't say that.

"I think you're right. I'll talk with the owner, and I'll let you know," is what he said.

This is a Friday afternoon, and I came to work Saturday morning at 8:30 a.m.; and as I was walking in the door, the owner was at the entrance. He shakes my hand.

"Congratulations! You're now my new sales manager. You're going to make more money. Life's going to be a little bit better."

Which, for the record, that's not really true. The money part is genuine, but your life gets a little more hectic when you step into these kinds of management positions, but it is something that I really wanted to do.

I remained a floor closer that day, and then I started training for my new position on Monday morning.

The truth is that, although I still needed some training, it's essential to understand that I was *always* preparing myself to be a sales manager the entire time I was a floor closer.

You've got to always prepare yourself for the next position that you're trying to get *before* you actually get it! I have a tough time trying to explain this to salespeople. This doesn't mean you just walk into the office of somebody who has a position that you want and get all up in their business. This means you need to be taking advantage of resources on the internet, learning how the position works, being observant, and understanding what the job entails before you actually get it. So that way, when you do have the opportunity to apply for that position, you're ready or very close to being ready.

I needed minimal training to become a sales manager. Ladies and gentlemen, becoming a sales manager in the car business typically takes five to ten years; I had accomplished this in eight months.

Sadly, the guy that I worked with and sat beside was let go only a couple of months after I was promoted. So here I am, by myself on the sales desk, working all these car deals, managing the sales team, putting in at least six solid days a week. We would ultimately go through, I think, seven sales managers before we found the right one. His name was also Brian, and he has become a good friend and sits beside me every day. He turned out to be precisely what the dealership needed, and quite frankly, exactly what I needed as someone to work with every day.

Before we hired Brian, I was promoted to the general sales manager. Some in the car biz have never achieved that position, but typically it takes ten years or more, depending on what dealership you're working at.

So now I'm the GSM.

There's only one position above that one, the general manager. It worked out great because I had been working with the GM since the day we opened the dealership. He and I have a great working relationship. And between the two of us, we battled through all the growing pains of Apex Imports. At this point, I've been with this dealership for almost five years, and it has been great. Part of my job is to train salespeople, oversee customer service, help with the finance management team, and write a sales curriculum.

I'm pretty good at it, if I say so myself!

Our numbers are good, our closing rate is excellent, our gross revenue is fantastic, but all of a sudden, I get this familiar old itch: I want to start stepping back out into the real world again. I'm not thinking about quitting my job, but I want to do something on the side because I've always had this entrepreneur side of me that needs to be fulfilled. And as Jim Rohn says, "Work full-time on your wages and part-time on your fortune."

Next Level Selling with Mad Mike

Several months back, as of writing this book, I started a podcast. Now, the truth is I probably should have created a podcast a decade ago. It is called *Next Level Selling*, and you can find it anywhere you listen to podcasts. If you don't listen to podcasts, maybe it's time you started! I keep the episodes ten to fifteen minutes in length because I wanted it to be something that people could listen to while they're driving to work, working out, or whatever. Even if you just have ten to fifteen minutes before you walk out the door, you can listen in nice bite-sized little pieces.

The goal is to give someone a shot in the arm, a little bit of motivation, selling tips, and teach them how to be a better salesperson—all while becoming a better version of yourself.

I personally believe that selling is all about mindset.

Yes, you need skills. There are techniques to be learned. Selling is a skill. Some people can seem to be born to do the job, but even those folks need training. You need to follow a process, and you need to learn proper techniques. I also don't believe that selling is about lying to people, cheating, stealing, or any of that crap. Selling is about educating your prospect, helping them understand what it is that they want, and helping them attain it. Whether it's a house, a car, or financial security, those are pretty much "needs." People need a place to live. In most cases, they need a car to drive, but regardless of what you're selling, you have to educate your prospect and help them understand *why* they need it. Overcoming whatever objections they may have, and overcoming an objection again, is simply providing more information to help the customer make an informed decision. I don't believe in hard closes. I don't believe in beating people over the head

—no arm twisting. I don't believe in lying to get them to make a decision, as that will *always* come back and bite you.

This is what I've done for years and years and years—decades even. I have sold products and services, tangible and intangible; I have gotten great satisfaction out of it. However, as I mentioned, when I was a stockbroker pitching stocks and bonds, I didn't really take pride in the money itself. I generated wealth all right, and some people think that making money is all life is about, but I assure you it's not. I prefer to make *good* money. I've lived with money, and I've lived without it, and I'm much happier with it, but it has to come from a place I am proud of. This, of course, is provided you gain satisfaction from how you actually *get* the money. When I sell a product or a service to somebody, and I get great satisfaction from what I'm actually selling, and the customer gets great satisfaction from the same thing, this is the key to sleeping well at night.

If you sleep well, then you will wake up feeling great about what you're doing! I'm helping people. I started my podcast *Next Level Selling* to reach out to help even more people, regardless of what they are selling. It can be real estate, cars, software, widgets, who knows; whatever somebody is selling, I feel like I have some information that could help them. And by no means am I saying that I'm the greatest salesperson of all time. There are some truly amazing salespeople out there. I listen to sales trainers all the time. I listen to personal development videos, coaching videos, motivational speakers, and I seek out information that can feed my brain to keep training, to improve even just a little bit every day.

And that's what I think everybody else could be doing too.

I simply want to be a part of this training world that helps people to become better salespeople by becoming a better version of themselves.

So yes, I guess I'm basically a motivational speaker at this point, but I do focus primarily on the mindset. And, if I'm picking a niche, then it's selling. But you don't have to be a salesperson to listen to my podcast: I promise you that.

So besides venturing down this road of doing my own podcast, I'm writing this book.

Hi!

I've already been approached by a few companies to come and speak for them, which really makes me happy. I guess my ultimate goal is to stand up in front of audiences once again and say words that could help them reach a new level in their life. Because I really do believe that this is the secret to happiness. That IS the secret to life, which is simply helping others. If you would reach out and help even one person, I think you'll find that the immediate gratification that you get from doing this is the most wonderful gift that you could give yourself, as well as others. I'll finish up with the starfish story, which I think is just a great analogy.

There's a girl walking down the beach one day, and there are thousands of starfish that have been washed ashore. As she's walking down the shoreline she picks up a starfish and throws it back into the ocean. She continues doing this one at a time. An older man is sitting up on the beach, watching her throw these starfish into the ocean. He walks up to her and says, "What are you doing? Don't you realize you can't make a difference by throwing these starfish back into the ocean? There's too many!"

And she reaches down, picks one up, and throws it into the ocean. "Well," she says, "it sure made a difference to that one!"

Do you understand where I'm coming from? Sometimes we get overwhelmed, thinking that we can't make a difference. I have had many friends and relatives die from cancer, and it is one of the worst diseases I think this world has ever faced. I wish I could do something to help them all, but the fact is that I can't. Hunger breaks my heart. As I'm writing this, statistically, eight thousand children a day die from starvation. I mean, this is a problem that we can cure with food, and it breaks my heart that we, as people, don't solve this problem. But I don't want to make this a political book. I don't want to make this about all of the terrible things that are going on in the world. I want to make it about what you and I can do as individuals to make a difference for even just one person.

149

CHAPTER 11: "JUST KIDDING, NO CHAPTER 11'S ALLOWED, TOO NEGATIVE"

CHAPTER 12: "THANK YOU"

Me; Now

Smile, Bow, Wave "Thanks for Being Here!"

You'll notice there's no chapter eleven in my book! To explain a joke kills the humor, but filing a Chapter 11 in the world of business is declaring bankruptcy (just for your continued education). Speaking what you want into existence doesn't mean burying your head in the sand and ignoring reality, although you need to BELIEVE that dreams really can come true! It means expecting the best and planning for the worst too. Talking something up but not following through with ACTION can give your speaking into existence lesson the opposite effect, so always make sure you're working toward your goals. Dare and be bold but don't be stupid, meaning always take calculated risks. Taking a leap of faith is fine, but make sure you have a reserve chute. Take the time to set up a net, attach a tether, and have a proper spotter! Unpacking that metaphor is to say when you take leaps of faith, make sure it's a loss you can afford or almost afford, that you have a plan B and, if at all possible, talk to people who've done it before. Do some "market research."

A "safety net" means not only keeping a portion of any investment portfolio stable with no/low-risk investments but making sure a lumpy revenue stream evens out once you have dependents. Even when we had stretched ourselves as far as possible to open that gym, I still had to mind the possibility of failure in regard to my growing family! Weigh the possibility of failure against the likelihood of success. In your drive toward a goal, don't lose sight of the ground beneath your feet. But be careful. All too often, we let fear of failure stop us dead in our tracks. Make no mistake, had ECB failed, then it would have been a major financial debacle. Regardless of knowing this possibility, I knew that not trying would hurt me down the road worse than the financial issue.

Suppose there's a single takeaway from all the chapters and all the thinking I've been doing on selling, not only the transactional sales you might be thinking of but persuading, influencing, and inspiring. In that case, it's that attitude really is everything. I can train you as much as you like, I can fill your head and condition your body, but you have to step in the door. You have to do the homework, and you have to basically, follow through. Just like so many sports: a strong follow-through is what it takes to win. So often, the victor is the one who showed up. And just showing up is 90 percent of success!

People love to dream, but only a few have the gumption to make it happen. Still, more folks love to shoot down those they see trying. Maybe it's envy; maybe it's the old "if I can't do it, you can't either" mentality. But in my experience, very few actually sign up and show up; most simply don't, and if they do, they give up. Of those who show up and start, many fall away. But not you.

Like the poster in my gym: crawl, puke, and cry, but *never give up.*

Always bite off more than you can chew and then chew like hell! I *should* make the title further convoluted and say, "spit something out before you choke." But that's the problem with trying to extend a metaphor too far; they all break down. Because biting and eating is a personal activity, after all, and service is such a large part of what makes us as human beings happy.

Always bite off more than you can chew and get involved with an organization helping cancer patients.
Always bite off more than you can chew and get involved in something that will make a difference in someone's life.

Always bite off more than you can chew and volunteer, coach, mentor, or find other ways to serve. Soup kitchens and homeless shelters, community gardens, or getting involved with your local food bank. Find something that fills your heart, and you'll have the other piece of the puzzle.

Science has shown us that love makes you live longer; happiness does too. Healing happens faster when you're not filled with stress and anxiety. We are social creatures, and anyone who lets themselves believe they hate everyone needs help! We're wired for society, literally evolved to be with other humans. Even if you're uninterested in intimate relationships, we all need a friend. People are socializing less and have fewer and fewer friends in the twenty-first century compared to previous ones, so it's worth dwelling on when considering your wants and needs.

Remember this: you may not be able to add years to someone's life, but you can absolutely add life to someone's years.

The prizes go to the ones who DO.

Now . . . get up and go for it because you ARE a Rock Star!

THE RANGER CREED

Recognizing that I volunteered as a ranger, fully knowing the hazards of my chosen profession, I will always endeavor to uphold the prestige, honor, and high esprit de corps of the Rangers.

Acknowledging the fact that a ranger is a more elite soldier who arrives at the cutting edge of battle by land, sea, or air, I accept the fact that as a ranger, my country expects me to move further, faster, and fight harder than any other soldier.

Never shall I fail my comrades. I will always keep myself mentally alert, physically strong, and morally straight, and I will shoulder more than my share of the task, whatever it may be, one-hundred-percent and then some.

Gallantly will I show the world that I am a specially selected and well-trained soldier. My courtesy to superior officers, neatness of dress, and care of equipment shall set the example for others to follow.

Energetically will I meet the enemies of my country. I shall defeat them on the field of battle, for I am better trained and will fight with all my might. Surrender is not a ranger word. I will never leave a fallen comrade to fall into the hands of the enemy, and under no circumstances will I ever embarrass my country.

155

Readily will I display the intestinal fortitude required to fight on to the ranger objective and complete the mission though I be the lone survivor.

Rangers Lead The Way!

— Ranger Handbook SH 21-76

CPSIA information can be obtained
at www.ICGtesting.com
Printed in the USA
LVHW080933240222
711905LV00001B/20